Baltimore

Association of American Geographers

Comparative Metropolitan Analysis Project

Vol. 1   Contemporary Metropolitan America: Twenty Geographical Vignettes.
          Cambridge: Ballinger Publishing Company, 1976.
Vol. 2.   Urban Policymaking and Metropolitan Dynamics: A Comparative Geo-
          graphical Analysis. Cambridge: Ballinger Publishing Company, 1976.
Vol. 3.   A Comparative Atlas of America's Great Cities: Twenty Metropolitan
          Regions. Minneapolis: University of Minnesota Press, 1976.

Vignettes of the following metropolitan regions are also published by Ballinger
Publishing Company as separate monographs:

- Boston
- New York-New Jersey
- Philadelphia
- Hartford-Central Connecticut
- Baltimore
- New Orleans

- Chicago
- St. Paul-Minneapolis
- Seattle
- Miami
- Los Angeles

Research Director:
   John S. Adams, University of Minnesota

Associate Director and Atlas Editor:
   Ronald Abler, Pennsylvania State University

Chief Cartographer:
   Ki–Suk Lee, University of Minnesota

Steering Committee and Editorial Board:
   Brian J.L. Berry, Chairman, University of Chicago
   John R. Borchert, University of Minnesota
   Frank E. Horton, Southern Illinois University
   J. Warren Nystrom, Association of American Geographers
   James E. Vance, Jr., University of California, Berkeley
   David Ward, University of Wisconsin

Supported by a grant from the National Science Foundation.

Baltimore

Sherry Olson
McGill University

Ballinger Publishing Company ● Cambridge, Massachusetts
A Subsidiary of J.B. Lippincott Company

This book is printed on recycled paper.

International Standard Book Number: 0-88410-440-0

Library of Congress Catalog Care Number: 76-4794

Printed in the United States of America

Library of Congress Cataloging in Publication Data

Olson, Sherry H
  Baltimore.

  Bibliography:
  1. Baltimore metropolitan area—Social conditions.   2. Baltimore metropolitan area—Population.   4. Urban renewal—Baltimore metropolitan area.   I. Title.
  HN80.B3037   309.1'752'604   76-4794
  ISBN 0-88410-440-0

Contents

List of Figures vii

List of Tables ix

A Baltimore Rhythm 1

Row House City 3

City of Neighborhoods 11

Rings and Wedges 17

The Tense Economy 31

Development and Redevelopment 47

Mobility and Uncertainty 63

City on the Falls 71

The Institutional Neighborhood 81

The Image: Does it Matter? 87

Bibliography 91

About the Author 95

List of Figures

1. Row House City   5
2. Town Housing in East Baltimore   7
3. Row House City and Suburban Dwellings   9
4. The Industrial Matrix of North Point Peninsula   12
5. Cold Spring Model   14
6. The Constellation, Moored in the Inner Harbor During the City Fair, 1973   15
7. Extremes of Mean Income Per Person   18
8. Use of Private and Parochial Schools, 1970   19
9. The Core Segregations—Poverty, Race, and Structural Dependency   20
10. Wedges by National Origin   24
11. Blue Blood and White Marble   25
12. Expansion of the Black Ghetto, 1950 to 1970   27
13. Racial Mobility in the Pennsylvania-Eutaw Corridor   28
14. White Collar and Blue Collar Workers at Home   36
15. Labor Force Stratigraphy   38
16. Metropolitan Labor Force by Race, Sex, and Occupation   39
17. Sparrows Point Steel Plant   41
18. Social Security Complex, 1973   42
19. Baltimore Harbor, 1973   48
20. Strategy and Tactics of Downtown Redevelopment   50
21. Charles Center, City Fair, 1973   51
22. Units of Public Housing and Households Displaced by Urban Renewal and Public Housing, Baltimore City, 1951-1971   54
23. Residential Turnover Outside the City   56
24. Median Value of Resident-Owned Homes, 1970   58
25. Rings of Residential Change in the City, 1960 to 1970   60
26. Migration Streams by Race, in Thousands of Moves During the Five Year Interval   67
27. The Journey to Work, 1960 and 1970   67
28. The Sump and the Alabaster City   69
29. Sedimentation in Baltimore Harbor   73
30. Dunbar High School   84
31. Downtown in 3-D   88
32. Kids Running, the Dome of City Hall, a Patchwork of Downtown Land Uses   89

List of Tables

1. Occupational Groups by Race and Sex, Metropolitan Area, 1970   43

Baltimore

A Baltimore Rhythm

Two million people, three-quarters of a million dwellings, 2,000 factories, 1.4 million acres of land—this is the Baltimore region. We have to imagine it in motion—two million trips a day, 150,000 people moving into the city to work and out again, 3,000 arriving or taking off at the airport; the never-ending flow on the beltway, in and out to Washington, in and out to Philadelphia; giant food trailers to the warehouses, containers to the port, ships loading for Japan and South America; five TV and twenty-six radio stations all talking at once; and, underneath, the hidden circulation of gas mains, taps running 250 million gallons a day, current flowing, millions of switches and thermostats and valves connecting nature with the comfort of the two million.

The rhythms of every day define the parts of the city. They define the downtown, alive at noon with secretaries under bubble umbrellas, at 2:00 P.M. with men in wilted shirtsleeves, alive with teenagers in the afternoon, and Hare Krishna, pencils for the blind, the *Watchtower, Muhammed Speaks,* the balloon man. The rhythms of every day define the inner city—red brick and white stoops like a gigantic sundial, with people sitting or shifting to follow the patches of shade; roller skates racing buses; crowds proportional to the density of ambulances or fire trucks; children getting louder and later as the summer wears on. And in the suburbs, lawn sprinklers, kids on bicycles, damp green evenings, the sound of mowers, the action at the shopping center.

The system seems not much different from any other "two million city." But this everyday movement has its own rhythm, its own pace, and in the unique site and climate they give Baltimore its character. Spring overwhelms all the gardens with azaleas and roses and lasts for three days in April. Summer lasts forever. Blue flax two feet tall takes over the strips between the concrete dividers, and the humid haze varies from Blue Ridge beauty to a yellowish temperature inversion where you smother in a flapping breeze, and skidding newspapers and litter map out the microclimate at ground level. The weekend is defined by massive exodus and reflux from the Eastern Shore and 100,000 boats on the Chesapeake Bay. Fall is golden clumps of beeches in the coves of Druid Hill Park, tall straight tulip poplar on the plateaus, the purple of sweet gum and dark green scrub pine on the sandy coastal plain south and east of town. Winter can never make up its mind—the weather changes every eight hours, but night falls at 4:30, and all the houses in the row show a little bluish light in the front rooms and a warm yellow light in the backs.

And the rhythms of everyday define who's who—a social circulation in which the work trips, the shopping trips, the auto trips, the bus trips, the phone calls are assigned to different people in different parts of town. The azaleas, the air conditioners, the litter all have their geography. Rich and poor, young and old, black and white. Crab imperial, steamed crabs, crabcakes.

As the year turns, the system itself grows— 100,000 new cars, 25,000 building permits, 28,000 real estate transfers, a thousand buildings torn down; $100 million for an express-way, $20 million for a shopping center, $10 million for a high school. Baltimore has doubled in the past generation (thirty years) and its geographical features have changed radically. The leading edge of change is now defining a new and still different city, on a new scale.

Row House City

First impression and most persistent image of home is always the rows of brick, one room wide, two or three stories, with white marble steps (Figure 1). Only 40 percent of the households in the metropolitan area live in single family detached dwellings. Perhaps another 10 percent live in high-rise buildings. Half live in row houses. To the visitor from the Midwest or farther away, the brick rows produce a feeling of monotony, a threat of anonymity, and the anxiety of getting lost in the maze. A view from the railway embankment as you come from Philadelphia is grimmer—the black tarred roofs sloping back to the alleys by hundreds and thousands. The streets run straight and suddenly go off at an unexpected angle. But the longer you live in Baltimore, the more variety, the more solidity, the more character the brick rows seem to acquire, until you know just where you are and where you're going.

First, you know where you are in terms of the growth of the city. Like other cities, Baltimore grew ring by ring, a building boom every twenty years or so, annexing territory, filling it up, spilling out. The styles of the row houses of each great building cycle define their location in one of these rings. We are situated in time—new city, hand-me-down city, third generation city. . . . The brick landscape can be read like a drill core of coastal plain sediments or geologic history in a roadcut. The oldest houses were narrow, ten or twelve feet, four rooms or six, with peaked roofs and dormer windows. Some ran back a hundred feet or

were three stories high. This central ring of housing is disappearing rapidly as renewal spreads. Its very core, the Inner Harbor district, has been renewed not once but several times— a massive warehouse construction in the 1880s, a total fire and reconstruction in 1904, and total clearance over the ten years ending in 1972.

The next zone, which seems immense if you're on foot, is the inner city, extending to North Avenue (on the north) and beyond Monroe Street on the west. It "filled up" in the great building boom of the 1880s. It is characterized by the wavy fronts, yellow brick facades among the red, and a dozen variations on the bay window. The city's size was doubled by annexing part of Baltimore County in 1888, and the rows marched on. After World War I came another annexation, and most of the porch fronts, with more stone, more stucco, and more frame. These are today's "pop art" facades, where the porch gable and roof pinions are shared by pairs and each owner paints his half a color that pleases him—triangles of yellow and green and white and brown marching over the crest of the hill.

After a long drought in residential construction during the Depression, and the cramped rows of war worker and public housing built during World War II, row house construction took new forms—the garden apartments, two, three and four story blocs often placed gable end to the street. From the late 1960s developers varied these with attached "town-

Figure 1. Row house city. Source: Baltimore City, Department of Housing and Community Development.

houses," staggered to avoid the severely uniform facade and variously painted, shingled, and picture-windowed.

Not only do you recognize where you are in the urban stratigraphy, but from the row house landscape you can read a social landscape: Where do you fit in an income-stratified society? In each era row houses have been designed for rich and poor. We have today the elegant townhouses of Cross Keys, a Rouse Company development, which rent for up to $1,000 a month, and the good-looking Broadway-Orleans townhouses of a municipal project which rent for $100. Back in the 1840s and 1850s the very rich occupied townhouses on Mount Vernon Place, Baltimore's elegant and unique cross-shaped park centered on the Washington Monument. These houses are wide and splendid

and most have been turned into clubs or institutions. Certain working class streets of the same era near the B & O railroad shops at Mount Clare have become hidden alleys of white poverty, persisting from one generation to the next. The narrower "interior" streets have wood stoops painted white to look like marble.

The social landscape can be wonderfully complicated because a different society has occupied rows designed for an earlier one. Many blocks laid out in the 1850s or 1860s, for example, were first occupied by well-to-do families in the three story rows fronting on the wider streets, and working class households in the two story fronts on the narrower cross streets and interior streets or alleys. Frequently "Anglo" households lived in the large houses,

Irish and German households in the lesser streets or alleys. After the Civil War, such interior streets were occupied mainly by blacks —waiters, laborers, laundresses, and servants in the big homes of "Anglo" families on Bolton Street or Park Avenue and, later, Jewish families on Eutaw Place.

But the wealthy class repeatedly abandoned its homes for something modern, leaving the larger structures to be cut up into rental units, commonly one per floor. The conversions account for the remarkable concentration of dwelling unit sizes in Baltimore City rentals in the category of three room apartments. The perennial exodus of the successful, and social renewal by immigration (from abroad, then from rural Maryland, and from North Carolina and Virginia), turned some of these social landscapes inside out. Near Broadway, for example, a stable group of middle-aged black homeowners occupy the smaller houses on the interior street (Eden), while the larger houses on the outside of the block are subdivided and occupied by white tenant families from Appalachian communities of western Maryland and West Virginia, and by Lumbee Indians from North Carolina.

In other areas, particularly areas of black residence for more than a generation, considerable diversity exists and the houses one by one show signs of status achieved, of aspiration, or of despair—lace curtains, flowered plastic, or tattered shades; African violets, petunias, or plastic carnations; Victorian oak entry or broken screen; the pink porch, the black and olive trim, or a thousand fingermarks.

Some social boundaries are scarcely visible in the physical landscape, but as a general rule the physical patterns and variations designed in earlier generations are differentially occupied and maintained. The scale, grain, and texture built into the landscape continue to provide the set of sieves by which today's society sorts people in terms of income, race, occupation, and age.

Rowhouse building was at the same time street making. Street making can be considered the fundamental urbanizing process. Each extension of the urban street system into new territory represents a structure that may stand for hundreds of years, although its surface is renewed often and the public utilities beneath may be rebuilt. Buildings, fine or ugly, well- or ill-built, may last fifty or a hundred years.

This has been described as the bony skeleton of our social capital, which is fleshed out by all manner of faster circulating capital—new vehicles and new façades, shed and renewed continually, like the skin—and the yet faster metabolism of energy and materials—paint, fuel oil, water, newsprint.

One of the pleasures of a row house city is the large number of streets which have a human scale. The 19th century city authorized streets to be graded and paved in orderly sequence, a few blocks at a time. The habit of builders was to create a row at a time, or facing rows. One finds many combinations arising from a few standard street widths with two, three or three and a half story rows and with certain designs and patterns to the façade. Some streets feel like paths or canyons, some like plazas; some are homey, some elegant. The presence or absence of street trees adds another variant and people in some neighborhoods scream for trees while people in others object just as vigorously to their presence.

Each great building boom was characterized by a new street-making strategy. In general, there has been a progressive shift to lower overall densities, larger developments, more street area per house, and heavier investment in the street-associated underground utilities (Figure 2). The ways in which the rows are put together further help to define where we are in time and space. The patching together of rectangular street grids independently laid out on the old irregular manor properties of Maryland (Timber Neck, Ridgely's Delight) produces seams in the street system and angled rows, puzzling to a visitor from rectangular survey states. The working class districts of the 1890s have factory chimneys at the ends of their streets, while the middle class 1890s have their skyline punctuated by corner turrets.

Convenience shopping is by definition closely associated with residences and is therefore part of the row-and-street structure. The corner store and corner tavern trace out the pre–World War I city. Certain larger commercial nodes, circles, and strips reflect a streetcar pattern and zoning strategy of the 1920s. The gas station corners trace out a post–World War II city. Each of these commercial patterns allied with residence has produced problems of adaptation. The corner store and corner bar represent nuisance as well as convenience. The corner bars and commercial strips were the locus of the 1968 looting and burning and we now have

Figure 2. Town housing in East Baltimore. Source: Baltimore City Department of Housing and Community Development.

incredible architectural adaptations of "forti-
fied" liquor caches. Gas stations have proved
exceptionally expensive to adapt to any other
use, to disguise, or even to demolish, and 250
derelicts remain in the city as relics of gas wars,
gas shortages, and the invasion of Baltimore by
multinational corporations.

With the annexation of 1888, as the city extended onto more rolling terrain and the upper
middle class bought into lower density "suburbs," the engineers came to grips with the
costs of paving, watering, and sewering it all.
They therefore abandoned the rigid grid street
plan and introduced a new sensitivity to terrain, building some fine viaducts, elm-lined
parkways, and winding rustic roads (for example Gwynns Falls Parkway and Windsor Mill
Road). The alley system was abandoned and
the old alleys were paved. The progress of the
automobile in the 1920s and again in the late
1940s fostered a preference for the dead-end
lane. The new scale of developers and cheapen-
ing of earth-moving favored immense grading
projects, and high and low priced postwar
developments can be differentiated by the
preservation of terrain, old trees, and vistas.
Each street-making strategy reflects a change
in the concept of an environment for living,
as well as changing notions of privacy.

DEPARTURES FROM THE ROW
HOUSE MODEL

What about the other half? We can treat the de-
partures from the row house model as two
basic types—the detached dwelling and the
apartment house.

Detached dwellings are more numerous,
about 50 percent in Baltimore County and 75
percent in Anne Arundel County, the major
new postwar suburban area (Figure 3). The
detached dwellings belong to a "village" style.
They are not truly rural in origin since the
Maryland landscape was one of plantations,
isolated farms (in the piedmont), and wide
places in the road rather than villages. Bits and
pieces of "string towns" or roadside relays
are found as nuclei, as at Waverly and Reisterstown. The omnibus, the horse railway, and a
steam commuter rail line made possible gentle-
men's villages like Mount Washington, Catonsville, Ruxton, and Lutherville. Marylanders who
could afford it adapted to the climate and its
health hazards by maintaining winter (town)

and summer (country) houses, as well as winter and summer rugs, drapes, and furniture.
By 1900 the existence of those villas and
villages, together with international trends
toward planned suburbs and the appearance of
the electric street railways, produced a new set
of villages designed for year round living of
upper middle class commuters—notably Roland
Park and Walbrook. In the 1920s the model was
extended to more modest classes, as at Dundalk
and Brooklyn, but a compromise was shaped
between the curving street and the row house.

Finally, after World War II, Baltimore participated in the national suburban development
boom. The vital elements, as elsewhere, were
the opening up of long term mortgages (FHA
guarantees) and the acquisition of automobiles.
We can map out the village model in terms of
the curves in street patterns. One of the more
comprehensively planned was Edmondson Village—around a "colonial" style shopping center, with a public library, school, etc. Single
family dwelling suburbs were seen as the modern way to live and symbolized the "anticity"
to which people leaving row house Baltimore
would flee. In the 1950s detached dwellings
were preferred by the affluent midwestern newcomers to central Baltimore County and the
somewhat less affluent newcomers from southern towns into Anne Arundel County. For
these outsiders, row housing was never identified with a middle class lifestyle. While hundreds of such "places" exist, distinctive as
Arbutus, Linthicum, and Pumphrey in one
small area, the suburban "villages" never pos-
sessed the sense of corporate solidarity of an
urban tradition. Social boundaries were maintained without legislative boundaries. The
counties do not contain incorporated towns
and cities such as hem in Cincinnati or Detroit.
Traditionally, the only important potential
boundary is the county line. The city has not
been part of Baltimore County since 1851.
They are independent jurisdictions and no annexation to the city has taken place since 1918.

APARTMENTS

Before World War I, when New York and
Chicago were building six story walk ups as
well as skyscrapers, Baltimore was building
six story warehouses, its skyscrapers could be
counted on one hand, and it took pride in having no tenements and an exceptionally large

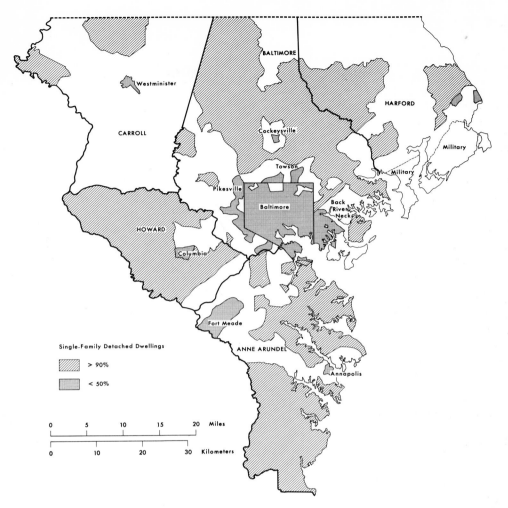

Figure 3. Row house city and suburban swellings. Only 40 percent of the region's housing units are single family detached dwellings, but they dominate a far greater portion of the region's land resource. The "row house" city is compact.

proportion of homeowners. Row housing, buttressed by a remarkable network of small mutual financial institutions and a British legal relic known as the ground rent (a family buys a home without buying the ground beneath), made homeownership cheap and popular and "stabilized" the working class.

In the 1920s new apartment houses and residential hotels of fifty to a hundred units were associated with grand views, pillars, and ballrooms. They were built on the new parkways or opposite city parks, as on Druid Park Lake Drive, Eutaw Street, Charles Street opposite Wyman Park, or the Mount Vernon area.

Many are now identified with shabby gentility, student ghettoes, or rip-offs of black tenant families who find themselves periodically without heat or hot water.

The next step in apartment construction was at the other end of the income spectrum. Wartime slum clearance projects were frustrated by the high densities per acre: planners could not rehouse the population and leave room to hang the laundry. About 1955 national prominence was given to ingenious designs for "high rise low cost" as at Pruitt-Igoe in St. Louis. Baltimore built in this style between 1955 and 1965 at central locations and the objections to this habitat have been felt here as elsewhere. In 1964 Baltimore's public housing authority recognized that these caged in environments were not suitable for families with children. They made a quick switch into high-rise apartment construction for the elderly in response to new federal housing subsidies. Public and nonprofit housing encountered much less resistance to the siting of apartments for the elderly—harmless and without automobiles—in contrast to all other low and moderate income populations. Therefore, we now see a curious sprouting of these high-rise buildings, ranging from plain to ugly, spotting the skyline of the city. These structures tend to house from 200 to 500 residents. Because federal regulations for their special funding are rigid in their income selectivity, they breed societies segregated by age and by income. There are 3,700 public units (low rent) and perhaps 2,000 nonprofit units (moderate rent).

Meanwhile, the same demographic trends, coupled with the rising value of land, new construction methods, income tax privileges, and the anxiety about violence, have favored the construction of high-rise communities for wealthier populations. Concentrated by zoning and parking regulations, several sizable apartment clusters have developed within the last ten years, including one at Towson (the capital of Baltimore County), one at the crossing of Reisterstown Road and Ford's Lane, and one north of the Johns Hopkins University campus along University Parkway and Charles Street. Investors have been extremely cautious with respect to luxury high-rise apartments in the downtown. There are clusters near Mt. Vernon Place and Charles Center, but "urban-oriented" professionals have also accomplished considerable reconversion and modernization of row houses. Favorite Sunday afternoon events in spring and at Christmas are "open houses" in renovation neighborhoods such as Bolton Hill, Charles Village, Federal Hill, and Fell's Point. The Baltimore rows continue to show remarkable adaptability for new lifestyles.

City of Neighborhoods

There are as many definitions of neighborhood as there are geographers, planners, and sociologists to debate them. Common notions include physical boundaries; a definite social network based on shared ethnic, cultural, or class identity; a sharing of certain facilities; and special emotional connotations. Neighborhoods combining all four elements, Suzanne Keller argues, are rare in modern cities.

But for some reason neighborhoods seem to be a real and universal phenomenon in the Baltimore region. I would attribute this to a remarkable correspondence of scale among physiography, the organization of the construction industry, pedestrian range, and the social units within which children play and grownups gossip and keep up with the Joneses. The elaborate and nearly indestructible differentiation of the physical landscape was the basis for gradual historical differentiation. Baltimore's topography also reinforces a strong distinction between walking spaces and riding or driving spaces, between neighborhood convenience stores and a regional shopping center or downtown, between neighborhood institutions and outside services, and between those who go outside to work and those who stay in the neighborhood in the daytime.

We are talking about a scale of ten to twenty blocks in the city, ranging up to 10,000 residents. In the counties the area probably ranges between half a square mile and a square mile. Is there any objective way to "find" such neighborhoods? Maps of street networks reveal several hundred small subsystems. In the outer ring of the city and in the suburban counties

highly connected nets appear, between which the only connection is a single link, a single through route, or a route with three or four entries. These are pedestrian nets joined by vehicular modes of travel. The rural-suburban edge can also be discerned. Within the city the grid is more completely connected, but one can nevertheless see unusual differentiation, with parks, watercourses and steep valleys tracing out barriers to everyday pedestrian movement. Industrial areas, highways, and railroads are perceived barriers, but historically their layout was also influenced by relief and drainage in the natural landscape.

Consequently, we can contrast the two major physiographic regions. In the coastal plain on the south and east, the *rivers* (tidewater inlets) dominate the shape of this isolation and differentiation of neighborhoods. The *necks* (peninsulas) govern the way roads and public utilities are laid out. Railroad yards and industrial proper-govern the way roads and public utilities are laid out. Railroad yards and industrial properties form barriers in this landscape and also contribute employment bases which give a certain cohesion to neighborhoods (see Figure 4). In the piedmont, the stream valleys are more often narrow, the land is rolling, and the controlling factor in construction and layout of roads is slope.

CONTROL BY DESIGN

On that complex natural foundation, cultural patterns were embroidered. In Baltimore the role of the large landowner, subdivider, or

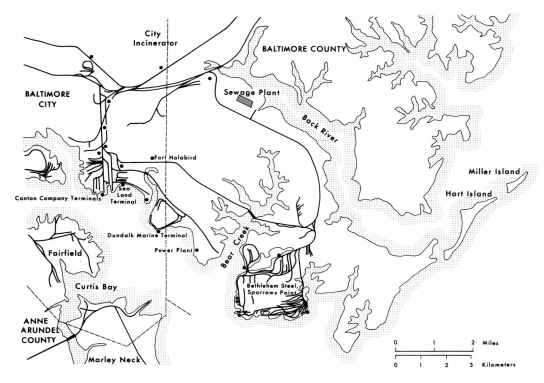

Figure 4. The industrial matrix of North Point Peninsula. Railroads ring the North Point Peninsula. Major industries form the rim on the North, West, and South. Along Back River are the city incinerator, land fills, the regional sewage treatment plant, and the islands scheduled for dumping of spoil from harbor dredging.

developer has always been important in the formation of neighborhoods. He transforms a marsh, a neck, or a hilltop into a neighborhood he believes will appeal to a certain market. His selection of price, location, and design creates a new social subsystem and a new bundle of property rights. The social system is vulnerable to change, as families grow up and regional housing market opportunities shift. But the people in the neighborhood generally want to maintain their social system—status, cultural group, and lifestyle. They develop institutions—formal or informal, legal or illegal—to protect the kind of neighborhood they have. Baltimore's scores of neighborhood improvement associations are a highly visible defense mechanism. So are local institutions such as school or parish, and shops which project a consistent market image. Less visible but important for perpetuating the social subsystem are the vested property rights and mechanisms for maintaining and transferring these rights. We

can get some idea of the variety of these mechanisms by looking at half a dozen communities, most of them along the Jones Falls valley between North Avenue and the city line.

One type of neighborhood social system based on property right is the company town. Over the nineteenth century, cotton mill owners developed strings of mill villages totaling 20,000 to 40,000 people along the mill streams or "falls". The easiest to visit are in the Jones Falls valley at Woodberry (below 40th Street), and downstream along Clipper Mill Road. These villages had a company store, Methodist chapel, and schoolhouse on company land and an occupationally structured arrangement of homes—stone duplexes for worker families, rooming house for single girls, detached dwellings with verandas farther up the hill for the supervisors' families, and, overlooking it all, the millowner's family mansion. For a hundred years they excluded sale of liquor and evicted residents who went on strike or took boarders not employed in the plant. The houses were sold off when cotton duck production declined in the 1920s. (In contrast, Bethlehem Steel has *consumed* its old company town at Sparrows Point for plant expansion.)

A variant is the "multicompany town" along the eastern city line. The Canton Company (incorporated 1830) progressively developed 3,000 acres by selling off waterfront lots for industry and inland residential building lots to housing developers. The plan assured a viable employment base for working class neighborhoods. The Canton Company retained the ground rents, and the various building and savings societies of the Polish, Bohemian, and German parishes enabled residents to buy up the rows of six room houses. Many homes have been inherited by a third generation. South of Patterson Park, for example, seventy and eighty year old brick houses with marble steps and stained glass lights shine like new all over, refitted with aluminum doors and windows and often with a patented imitation stone veneer.

New corporations in the 1890s adopted a strategy of developing purely residential neighborhoods. The Western Maryland railroad developed Sudbrook with F.L. Olmsted as architect. The Roland Park Company laid out a prestige community on the hills north and east of Woodberry. A commuter rail line, a private water company, large lots, a fine designer and architects, the rugged terrain, and an exclusive social group. The corporation structured the community through clauses in the contracts of sale and real estate deeds, to prevent commercial uses; the building of fences, walls, or additions; and occupancy by Negroes and Jews. They also required that property owners participate in a corporation of residents and levied a tax for certain services of street cleaning and maintenance. Over forty years they gradually extended their building strategy to other large tracts across the northern tier of Baltimore City (Guilford, Homeland, and Northwood). They adapted the devices to varying income levels.

The way in which the corporate developers of the elite neighborhoods planned and managed their communities reveals the pecking order of Baltimore society. The order of priorities, as worked out in practice, appears to have been the exclusion of blacks, the exclusion of Jews, and the exclusion of Catholic Europeans. The exclusion of people less affluent than the local norm overlapped with the other goals and the two conceptions were mutually reinforcing —social exclusion in order to protect homeowners' property values and economic barriers to insure social exclusiveness.

Naturally, as their economic conditions improved, excluded groups organized to create their own building and loan societies, build their own neighborhoods, and make them exclusive, too, further differentiating social areas and reinforcing a generalized pecking order. In this sense, Baltimore is a city of several hundred ghettos, each a little different.

Even where developers sold off all their property rights, a social subsystem could be maintained by mechanisms for limiting the homeowner transfer of property rights. In Hampden, on the plateau east of Woodberry and south of Roland Park, this applies to both homeowner and rental housing. Homeownership at workingmen's prices was coupled with a system for sifting and financing the entry of acceptable (white) replacement buyers through neighborhood realtors and savings and loan companies of local identity. Before World War II a large share of the still more modest rental homes were owned by several storekeepers on the "main street"; the Hampden bank was their principal lending institution. The relation of the neighborhood bank, a miniature downtown, the interlocking ownership of property and enterprise, and the manipulation of social structure are features of a model repeated in other neighborhoods, such as Highlandtown on the east, Little Italy near the center, or Glen Burnie in the suburbs.

Overall, this system produced certain painful contradictions. Because the choice of blacks in particular was so restricted, the black housing market became a pressure cooker. Blacks had to pay more for equivalent space, but whites would pay more for solid or "safe" property than for mixed or fringe blocks. These price differentials were incentives for realtors to organize the turnover of blocks or neighborhoods, one by one, at a rate that would just maintain the pressure. The process can be observed from 1900 down to the present moment. Only in the late 1960s did Maryland courts and the legislature begin to interfere in certain practices regarded as "private" property law—the restrictive covenant on the buyer's future resale, the owner's right to choose a buyer, the realtor's right to solicit business or steer potential buyers to acceptable areas, and the apartment owner's right to discriminate in renting and leasing.

New mechanisms, less racist and less explicit, are being developed to stabilize and protect a differentiated social structure and a neighborhood scale within large developments. In their village of Cross Keys, the Baltimore-based Rouse Company employed a high rent, long lease strategy. The village was built in the 1960s on the former golf course of the Baltimore Park Country Club, just north of Woodberry. Income exclusion remains solid, although great pains were taken to avoid racial exclusion. Partly on this prototype, Rouse planned the much larger "new town" of Columbia in Howard county. It is composed of residential villages, or neighborhoods, walkways and open space, industrial park, and town center. It already has 35,000 people, and is designed for 100,000.

The latest innovation is a joint plan of city government and private enterprise for Cold Spring, a "new town in town" for 12,000 people on a 500 acre quarry west of Jones Falls and just opposite Cross Keys. In the design Moshe Safdie (architect for Habitat in Montreal) uses a three dimensional concept of neighborhood, with clusters of high-rises and villages of townhouses (Figure 5). Lawrence Halprin, landscape architect, was involved, to protect the adjoining nature park (Cylburn) and develop the environmental assets—exceptional amounts of open land and vistas of the

Figure 5.   Cold Spring model. Photo courtesy of Moshe Safdie, Architect.

Figure 6. The Constellation, moored in the Inner Harbor during the City Fair, 1973. Photo by Jim Kelmartin, *Baltimore News-American*.

rugged landscapes, natural and manmade. The developer is a Connecticut corporation, but some federal financial participation is assured to permit a wider, less exclusive range of rent levels. Rents must at the same time pay for a high quality physical environment and insure a sufficiently stable and protected social environment to attract people of that range of incomes.

Observers have suggested that there are signs of a renaissance of neighborhood, as there was in Baltimore in 1908–1910. Small neighborhood associations have become more numerous, won more legal and political victories, and formed large regional coalitions. As in other cities, neighborhood associations have—here and there—received support from the housing and urban renewal agency which assigns com-

munity organizers and the planning department which assigns district planners. Poverty and model cities programs seeded new neighborhood organizations in the inner city. A symbolic representation of this was the creation in 1970 of the September Baltimore City Fair. Modeled on the old-fashioned three day country fair, it has been enormously successful, attracting hundreds of thousands (Figure 6). Neighborhood associations annually take booths in which to sell their cookies or welcome mats, and with them their messages, political goals, and a neighborhood image. Nevertheless, the limited effectiveness of neighborhood defense strategies indicates the existence of powerful forces antagonistic to neighborhood. These forces determine the large scale segregations which are the subject of the next chapter.

Rings and Wedges

From the maps one can see a system of oppositions in the fabric of the metropolis. Among the most striking are maps of race, income, and private school attendance (Figures 7, 8, and 9). These are maps real and familiar to Baltimoreans. Many can draw these boundaries more consistently than the boundaries of their own "neighborhoods," and more accurately than they can map the major street pattern. Taken together, they map out deep-seated fears, envy, and mistrust. These tensions—open or concealed, conscious or unconscious—make the encounters of individuals in various parts of town comfortable or uncomfortable experiences that in turn generate a sense of security or anxiety about probable future encounters. On the basis of such expectations, people choose or avoid certain routes, locations, or trips in their everyday behavior, and so reinforce the boundaries and oppositions.

The three variables mentioned show extreme polarization. For example, most census tracts are nearly all black or nearly all white. Most individuals are socially defined as belonging to one of two "races," and two-thirds of all census tract populations are more than 90 percent of one race or the other. Likewise, the people of a census tract are either substantial users of private schools or they are not: only seventeen tracts out of 350 have more than 10 percent of their elementary children in private schools, but in half of these the figure is over 30 percent. Private schools, as classed in the U.S. Census, are distinguished from parish schools. Most of the parish schools are Catholic, but there are also Catholic private schools. Most tracts have figures under 1 percent. If we compare the frequency distribution of mean income by tracts with the overall income distribution of individuals in the total metropolitan area, they are much alike. This implies a high degree of spatial sorting by income. Most of the people in the "tails" of the distribution—the rich and the poor—must be living in different areas from everyone else.

The patterns of the maps make it clear that these polarities form large spatial discontinuities. They can be thought of in terms of the traditional urban patterns of ring and wedge—a black inner ring or core and a high income wedge in which many children go to private schools. A high income wedge is a feature Hoyt described in the 1930s for thirty American cities, and ring structures have proved basic in all urban multivariate analyses. It is likely that the unusually successful "tracting" of Baltimore and the strength of its neighborhood structure produce easier to read patterns than most cities. While Baltimore's pecking order may be more rigorous, it does not differ fundamentally from other U.S. cities. We will show here how the two sets of phenomena—rings and wedges—are related.

THE RINGS

The same variables which reveal neighborhood differentiation also reflect this larger scale op-

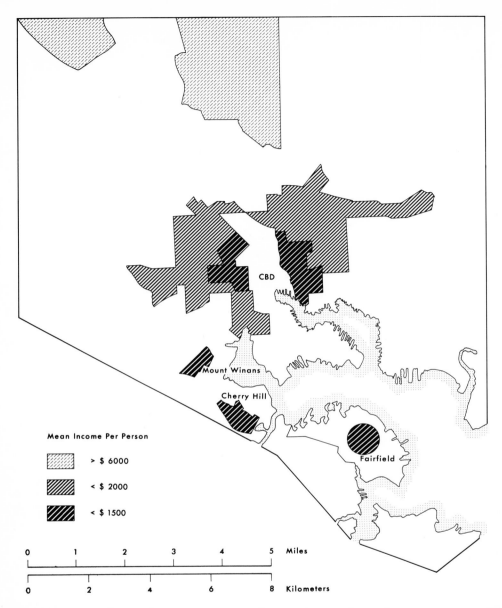

Figure 7. Extremes of mean income per person. Average income for each man, woman, and child in a tract shows the wedgelike distribution of the rich (over $6,000) and the inner ring of poverty (under $2,000). Public dependency is powerfully segregated: the lowest incomes (under $1,500) in the city are found in concentrations of public housing, and in the counties in institutional populations—state hospitals and prisons. Data for 1969.

position. For example, while there are dozens of distinctive black neighborhoods, most are grouped together into a black core or inner city. This core exists entirely within the city of Baltimore and is surrounded by a narrow, uneven, and fragile margin of change and an all-white periphery on the north, east, and south.

There has always been geographical expression of race discrimination in Baltimore. In the eighteenth century it was at the household scale—servants' dwellings over the backyard brick kitchens. In the nineteenth century it was at the row and alley scale of the city block. Three small black neighborhoods of the 1850s

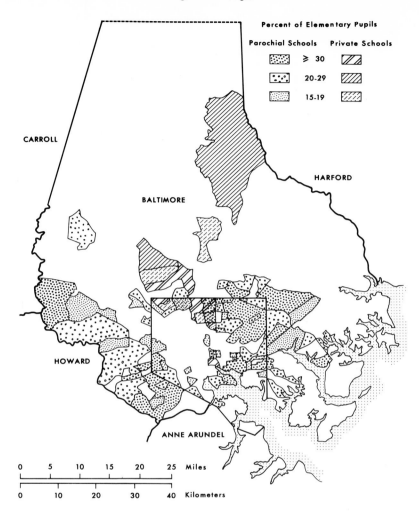

Figure 8. Use of private and parochial schools, 1970. A northern wedge of private school users overlaps on the east a wedge of Catholic parochial school users. A Jewish corridor (see Figure 10) overlaps the wedge of private school users on the west. Users of "parochial schools" in the northwest corner of the city are users of Jewish schools.

grew from narrow streets and alleys. They expanded before World War I (compare W.E.B. Dubois), and by 1935 there was a three-lobed "ghetto," defined by the city fathers as a "ring of blight" around the central business district (The South Baltimore black ghetto has been virtually demolished.) But it is only in the postwar period that immense opposition to racial segregation has emerged at the scale of the metropolis. It has crystallized into a formal political opposition—Baltimore City 45 percent black, Baltimore County 3 percent black. In the metropolitan area, 86 percent of the black population (five out of six persons) live in the city, of the white population 31 percent. A second major ring distribution is what sociologists or human ecologists sometimes call familism. It appears in factor analyses of nearly all North American census data as a multivariate dimension. It amounts to a concept of "standard family"—two parents and their children. Census data give us only a few clues to this structure, but it is an important contrast between city and suburb. We find that primary individuals (men or women living alone) are over 8 percent of the city population, but only 3.5 percent of the suburban population. To put it another way, one person

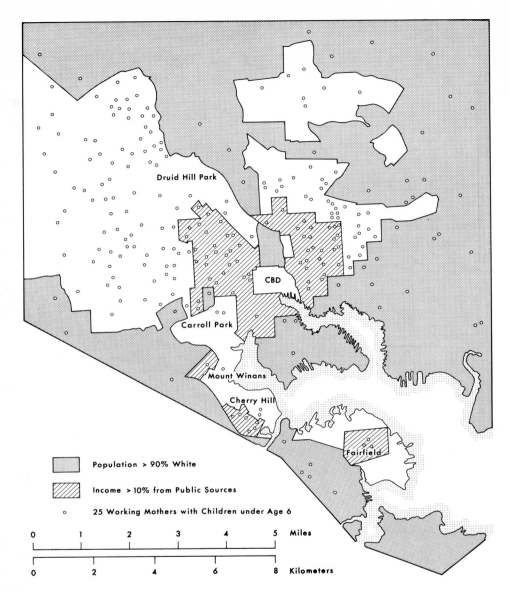

Figure 9. The core segregations—poverty, race, and structural dependency. Income from public sources includes social security, aid to dependent children. Because these incomes are low, in areas where they constitute over 10 percent of the total income the mean of the entire population must be low. The presence of working mothers with young children indicates a need for day care, but is correlated with inability to pay for it.

households are a quarter of all households in the city, but less than an eighth in the counties. Boarders and minors not living with either parent are twice as common in the city.

City-county differences in the percentage of women working outside the home are small, but this hides some important variations of work roles in relation to family life stages. Women with preschool children (under six) are only half as likely to work as women with school age children, grown-up children, or no children. In the two suburban counties, about one-quarter of the women with preschool children work; in the city 40 percent. The difference lies in the concentration in the city of black households in which the mother is much more likely to be in the labor force—half the mothers of preschool children (twice as many) and 62 percent of the other women. These figures apply regardless of whether the husband is present and reflect one of the ways in which the black family makes ends meet in spite of the lower average earnings per worker and more variable employment under "last hired, first fired" conditions. Labor force participation of white women is virtually the same in the city as in the suburbs.

ELEMENTS OF EXPLANATION

Row by row, neighborhood by neighborhood, the city pushed out from the core, influenced by great national booms of investment and tides of immigration. This kind of tree ring growth produced a ring structure of obsolescence at the center and, combined with the elaborate pecking order in Maryland society, organized a differentiation of the rings by race and income. Given also the high residential and job mobility of persons between eighteen and thirty-five, and their role in family formation, it might also produce the tendency toward rings in age distribution—young families in the new housing at the periphery, middle-aged settled families in intermediate rings, and the older generation in the center.

But that was a 200 year process. Other factors must be introduced to explain the new massive polarizations of the postwar years. The new phenomenon is the suburb. We have mentioned local suburban prototypes of the 1890s and 1920s, but massive suburban development was unleashed in Baltimore and Anne Arundel counties at the end of World War II. Rapid suburbanization resulted from a combination of technological change and social aspirations—an ideology of family life, the family automobile, the family-owned home, and the one family detached dwelling. These variables are geographically tied together in a suburban lifestyle. For example, outside a very small redeveloped center, there is an *old city* in which more than 80 percent of housing in every census tract dates from before World War II. The old city is belted by a narrow irregular zone in the annex of 1888, where the relief varies and radial routes pulled settlement into corri-

dors. Around that is a broad and more continuous belt (the 1918 annex) in which less than 45 percent of dwellings are prewar. Most of these date from the boom of the 1920s. In the ring beyond that (two suburban counties) only 20 percent of dwellings are prewar.

The construction rings match closely the rings of present-day automobile ownership. Throughout the new annex three-quarters of all households have automobiles. And in the suburban counties, the basic design or strategy of development has made it almost impossible to function without a car, and households without cars rarely reach 10 or 15 percent. In Baltimore County 45 percent of the households have two or more cars.

In the 1920s, detached dwellings distinguished middle class from working class districts. The value system which preferred detached homes, private yards, the private family car, the nuclear family with two or three "planned" children and a "full time" mother existed full blown before the war. But after World War II it suddenly became possible for great numbers of people to realize this aspiration. As cars became cheaper, as factory workers' incomes rose, as more women took jobs, the suburban ideal became a realistic goal of more people. Wartime conditions had forced people to save money; then installment buying was invented. Also essential were federal strategies to insure massive private investment in long term home mortgages, homeowner income tax incentives, and massive public investments in road building.

Development of housing at a scale of scores and hundreds of dwelling units was not a new phenomenon in Baltimore as it was in many cities, but, because of the lower density, the new wave of construction required assemblage of large tracts of open land. It did not therefore fill in the old city, nor extend from block to block as row housing had done.

As the new low density developments spread, decentralization of shopping and jobs followed swiftly. The public transit system collapsed into a shell and none was extended into the new districts. The state legislature gave new charter powers to the suburban counties to provide urban amenities such as water and sewers, fire protection, and modern schools. Political development of the counties has followed in the wake of their economic development.

THE LOGIC OF DEPENDENCY

Suburbanization seemed to offer a new opportunity to all, but it nevertheless left some people behind—those unable to drive, those whose life expectancy or income expectancy would not appeal to the mortgage bank, and those who, not being part of a family, would not place a high priority on the standardized three bedroom house and yard. In other words, a development strategy aimed at the standard family market implied the neglect of another large and growing group of people peripheral to this family. Spatially, the development of the postwar suburban ring implied the simultaneous "undevelopment" of an inner city ring. The geographical reorganization followed a rigorous logic of dependency.

Dependency is the way in which a society defines the relation between its producers and its "nonproducers." In an individualistic society based on individual producers, all nonproducers are considered dependents and are divided into two groups. Insofar as possible, they are assigned to individual producers as "private dependents" and we have the family as the basic unit of consumption, redistribution, and reproduction of society. Those who cannot be assigned to families become "public dependents" and are regarded as a tax burden shared by all producers. As we shall see, this ideology is the basis underlying the new postwar ring segregations. Family type dependency is concentrated in the suburbs and public dependency in an inner ring of the old city.

Within the family relationships are considered noneconomic, although the producer role has much to do with the forms of domination which occur. In recent years the burden has shifted to a smaller number of dependents for each producer, but a heavier per capita investment in the rearing and education of each child for a longer period before he enters the labor force. The geographical concentration of families in the suburban zone is associated with heavy capitalization of the family, heavy investment in the new generation, and a new degree of isolation of the family on its individual piece of ground. As we have seen, its low density on the land is associated with the use of a family car (or two) and is unfavorable to mass transit. In other words, it offers a sense of mobility and choice within—and only within—that transport mode. This lifestyle also implies a heavy affec-

tive load—or intensity of emotional relationships—within this small family structure. A sense of choice, mobility, and emancipation from one's parents is built into the mechanism of living in nuclear families. It provides the ties that hold the nuclear family together and the tensions that threaten it and at the same time reduces ties with the grandparent generation.

Meanwhile, in the core city, we see the segregation of public dependents, with high concentrations of "unrelated individuals" and nonproducers. Of the thirty-seven census tracts in which public transfer payments (social security, railroad retirement, aid to the aged, and aid to dependent children) exceed 10 percent of total income, thirty-four form a compact core. The other three are outlier neighborhoods of poverty, also in Baltimore City—Cherry Hill, Fairfield, and Mount Winans (evident in Figure 7). In the poverty core, we have 7 percent of the population of the metropolitan area, 7.5 percent of the housing units, but only 3.3 percent of the area's income. The income per person in this core is only $1,600, about half what it is in the remaining ring of the city and surrounding counties. The poverty arises from structural dependency. In this population, 9 percent are over sixty-five, 40 percent are under eighteen, and 12 percent (a quarter of the remaining producer-aged population) are at least partly disabled. In the region as a whole there is one dependent for each producer, but in this core there are two dependents for each producer. In fact most are nobody's dependents. As they do not have personal ties to individual producers, there is no personal sense of responsibility for their support and they receive smaller shares than private dependents in the overall social redistribution.

The stronger the family values and the pressures to invest in each child, the more families have tended to slough off their high cost dependents, particularly those who do not promise any return as future producers—for example, the physically or mentally disabled, the elderly, handicapped children, and those who are rebellious or ungrateful. The justification is that of a "normal" burden of dependency in relation to other producers in the society. For example, the retarded child is often institutionalized in order not to divert scarce resources from the child with greater potential. The number of public dependents therefore grows, and various classes of producers debate their shares of the burden of supporting them. This tends to reduce their maintenance. Regardless of where they are located, these dependents are more likely to be poor, as are half the "unrelated persons" over sixty-five. Of "poor" families, half have a woman as head of household (Figure 9).

But this squeeze makes it necessary to isolate the poor. Geographical separation makes the enormous differences of living standard less visible. The mean income of one census tract may be ten times that in another, but such tracts are separated by buffer zones, with continuous income gradients. The poor are not mobile and are not likely to be seen far from home; the 7 percent in the poverty core have a quarter of the carless households in the region. The wealthy have no reason to frequent the homes of the poor, as the homes of the poor have been gradually eliminated from the central business district itself, the suburban residents are doing more of their shopping in suburban shopping centers. In the five suburban counties, many of the poor are institutionalized. The only county tracts with per capita incomes as low as the core are the large state institutions for public dependents—those officially criminal, insane, retarded, or senile.

Geographical separation makes it easier for the majority in families to perceive the minority of public dependents as "other"—as a moral threat to the family as well as an economic burden, undeserving of any greater living standard. The core of Baltimore City is shared by greater than average proportions of abandoned wives, unwed mothers, the unemployed and the underemployed, the scarred and maimed, high school dropouts, alcoholics, old people, and communes. That is, geographical containment of various rejected populations produces a kind of moral contamination among the several groups as seen from the outside. A further guarantee of the sense of "otherness" is that the core population is 84 percent black. This makes it easier for the white suburban resident to resist any identification—"It's not *my* grandmother."

The poverty core is a human floodplain, where disaster strikes frequently and people are exceptionally vulnerable. Regardless of willingness, the capacity for mutual assistance is limited. Three-quarters of the households have no car (tracts range from 67 to 92 percent), and two-fifths have no phone. Any breakdown of the postal service or public agency accounting machinery delays public transfer payments to 10 or 15 percent of the population and in some tracts withholds up to 25 percent of the total income of the area. Not only do bureaucratic catastrophes occur, but victimization is heavily concentrated here for fraud, violence, and theft. The demographic structures make this population even more vulnerable. The ratio of male to female runs as low as 75 to 100. Relatively low birth weights and high death rates of infants indicate the chains of secondary effects at the extremes of vulnerability.

The short-lived "War on Poverty" (1962–1972) and Model Cities programs (1967–1972) zeroed in on essentially the core area described here and attacked some of the problems. For example, a strategy of distributing free iron-enriched infant formula is credited with reducing infant mortality and anemia. Some day care and job training centers allowed women and ex-prisoners to get jobs and the banks were persuaded to cash public assistance checks. Social service jobs allowed some individuals and households to escape the poverty area and the programs reinforced citywide black political efforts to fight job and housing discrimination. But the situation in the core area itself is probably worse than before. The underlying problems of structural dependency remain, and inflation, increased property taxes, and interest rates have raised rent and food costs. Since 1950 the trend toward elimination of large chain food stores in the center city has virtually run to completion, while the small, higher cost "Ma and Pa" stores have been decimated. As consumers, core residents not only have too few dollars, but their dollars buy less than other dollars because they are a concentrated and captive market. This is also characteristic of the three outlier areas where there are also more women and children, fewer cars and stores.

THE GREEN WEDGE

If the core of poverty is a circle, wealth is a wedge. Where the circle is the shape of immobilization, the wedge or radial is the shape of mobility. In looking at the wedges in the Baltimore area, we find that they always indicate mobility and that geographical movement along these radials has been associated with

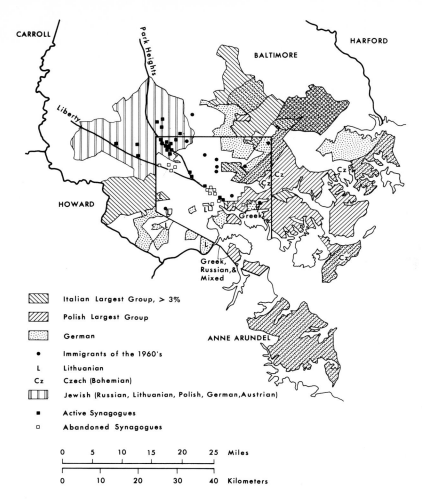

Figure 10. Wedges by national origin. Locations of synagogues show the radial path of the Jewish community, complicated by religious differences and place of origin. For example, in the northwest corner of the city along Park Heights there are numerous Orthodox congregations of German origin, while the Liberty Road corridor includes more households of Reformed, as well as nonreligious and Gentile communities. A former Litvak congregation was located near the earliest settlement of Lithuanian Catholics. Concentrations of immigrants of the 1960s (one dot for 300 persons) occur near hospitals and universities and include a large share of Asians. Sources: Joseph Feld; Census of 1970.

upward social mobility from one generation to the next.

The high income wedge of classic type is a solid chunk as shown by the mean per capita income contour of $6,000 (Figure 7). It coincides with the private school users (Figure 8). The origin of the wedge lies, historically, in the present-day banking district of the downtown, where merchant families had their homes and counting houses, then "uptown" in the court

house vicinity or government district of the city, then in the Mount Vernon area around the Washington Monument and Bolton Hill (Figures 10 and 11). The wedge extends into Baltimore County. It is possible to say that the city is polarized into rich and poor, while the county is polarized into rich and middle income —a split which appears in the political life of the county. The creation of Roland Park (the point of the wedge on the income map of

Figure 11. Blue blood and white marble. Radial mobility of families in the Social Register is shown by the difference of shading of street networks. Between 1912 and 1932, the streets in the older section (right figure, light lines) lost families, while the Roland Park Company suburbs (Roland Park, Guilford, and Homeland) gained. Figures in right hand map report by postal zone the number of Social Register families remaining in 1969. Of nearly 1,800 families in the register in 1969, all but a dozen lived in the towns and neighborhoods on these two maps, plus twenty-eight in Annapolis. Residential concentrations of Social Register families in Baltimore County show a linear pattern associated with two early commuter railroads which followed the valleys of the Jones Falls, Gunpowder Falls, and Gwynns Falls, and with the valleys developed on limestone. Marble is quarried near Cockeysville and Texas for the white stoops of Baltimore. It was used for the Washington Monument (Mount Vernon Place) and the marble trim on the surrounding homes. Source: Research by Mark Fleeharty.

1970) was the beginning of attention to "green" residential planning and respect for the admirable natural landscape. But with the exception of the century old city parks—Druid Hill, Clifton, Patterson, and Carroll—and its stream valleys, it has left the greening of Baltimore to the private market and the distribution of grass is the same as the distribution of greenbacks. Wealth is a wedge, poverty a circle. Likewise, green is a wedge and brick is a circle. Startlingly perverse is the distribution of air conditioners. If we consider the effects of natural terrain and microclimate, the effects of density and type of construction, there is no question that the heat dome of Baltimore centers over the poverty core. Here 9 percent of the households have air conditioners, while in the suburban ring over half do, and the percentage in tracts of the green wedge ranges between 65 and 99 percent.

The rent burden also has a perverse distribution. Average rents for dwelling units appear to be high in the central business district and low in the surrounding core, rising outwardly by rings. But if we consider variations in unit size and the frequency of homeownership, the wedge effect is evident, and if we look at rent in relation to income, the poverty core bears the heaviest burden. Perennial inequities in the property tax structure reinforce this burden. City tax rates are high, county tax rates lower, and within the city a 1974 study showed that properties in the green wedge were appraised for tax purposes below their market values, while inner city houses were overassessed.

ETHNIC WEDGES

We have already seen the striking central ring concentration of the black community, but one can also discern within it processes of radial mobility and a recent wedge or radial of extension toward the west, essentially the higher income movement along Druid Hill Avenue, then Ashburton and Forest Park, and out Liberty Heights Avenue and Liberty Road— the only sector in which we see a new concentration of black residents in Baltimore County (Figure 12 and 13). All the other enthnic groups show definite wedge structures. In fact, there exists a complete system of ethnic variations: everybody has a piece of the pie. This does not quite jibe with traditional descriptions of multiple nuclei of ethnic groups. Nevertheless, it is possible that a simple "Baltimore model" may apply to other cities. This dynamic model we might call a process of radial mobility.

The "ethnic wedges" are rather complicated to analyze because the census gives us not religion, but national origin, and national origin only in terms of first (foreign-born) and second generations. Each ethnic group has a different immigration history and a different balance of first, second, and third generations, etc. By examining in conjunction maps and

statistics of national origin, users of Catholic parochial schools, and the historical location of synagogues, we can trace out a process (see Figures 8-10). In the first generation we observe elaborate segregation by language and economic level, with a high concentration in the center city. In a second or third generation there is occupation of a larger area, farther from the center but still along an ethnic radial, with a greater mix of national origins but remaining within a higher order segregation by religion. This is consistent with sociologists' observations of "social distances" among such groups (Laumann) and it suggests that the notion of nuclei is illusory.

There exists a single broad wedge of Jewish settlement. Of the metropolitan region's 106,000 Jews, at least 90 percent live in this wedge. "Foreign stock" runs 20 to 40 percent (First and second generations), with a consistent national origin profile of Russian, Polish, Lithuanian, German, Austrian, and Rumanian in that order. The original heart of this corridor is eclipsed by recent black migrations, but can be seen in the presence of Jewish storekeepers and property owners and in the lovely restored building of one of the nation's oldest synagogues, on Lloyd Street near East Lombard. East Lombard Street is still the city's delicatessen row. The second foyer, in the Eutaw Place sector, is visible in the last remaining doctors' offices and a series of handsome synagogues, now Baptist and AME churches. The German Jewish immigrants who traced this path are also statistically erased because they are now in a third or fourth generation. In the early twentieth century a painful effort was made gradually to close the gap between highly educated and successful German Jews and the more recently immigrated East European Jews. The old differentiation of turfs between the groups is no longer apparent, but the Jewish wedge is extremely compact and extends into Baltimore County, where it is known as the Golden Ghetto. Jewish tenancy and ownership are still restricted from many other parts of the region. Two-thirds of the respondents in a study by Associated Jewish Charities described their neighborhood as all Jewish or mostly. Most expressed satisfaction with it "as is," not wishing it to be any "less Jewish."

The same study allows us to see how radial mobility produces both an ethnic wedge and a generational ring structure. It allows us to

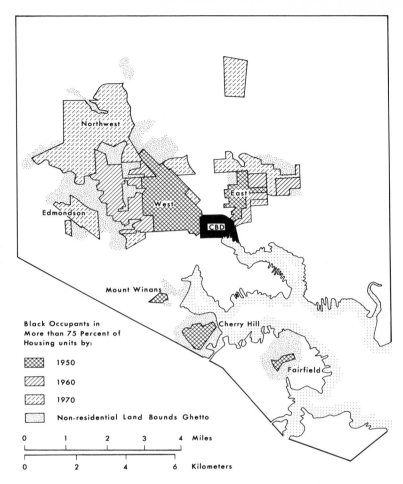

Black Occupants in More than 75 Percent of Housing units by:

1950

1960

1970

Non-residential Land Bounds Ghetto

0   1   2   3   4   Miles

0   2   4   6   Kilometers

Figure 12. Expansion of the black ghetto, 1950 to 1970. The boundaries are defined arbitrarily as black occupancy of more than 75 percent of the dwelling units in census tracts. Stippling shows where the ghetto is bordered or contained by nonresidential land uses.

relate the process of intergenerational social mobility. In the twenty-five to forty-four age group, college graduates are 27 percent of the population, double the percentage in the generation forty-five to sixty-four (14 percent). Of the present college age generation (eighteen to twenty-one), 85 percent are actually in college. A full range of housing types can be found in the wedge, but home-ownership rises from 15 to 84 percent outward along the wedge, while length of residence declines. The sections outside the city contain two-thirds to three-fourths "standard families" with concentrations of young children, while the inner areas contain more of all other household types, more elderly, and more foreign born.

One can discover a very broad sector of Catholic occupancy, from due north clockwise around to the southeast, and a second wedge in the west and southwest. Within these sectors there are further discernible districts—several distinctively Italian wedges, a broad single wedge of Polish settlement, and extensive German Catholic neighborhoods, with considerable mixing along the fringes. Concentrations of a single national origin were strongest in old central locations or hearths, but some have disappeared. The importation of German-speaking priests to serve German Catholics (1840s) and the creation of "national" parishes, with parish schools and savings societies—five Polish, two Bohemian, one Lithuanian, several Italian—reinforced and

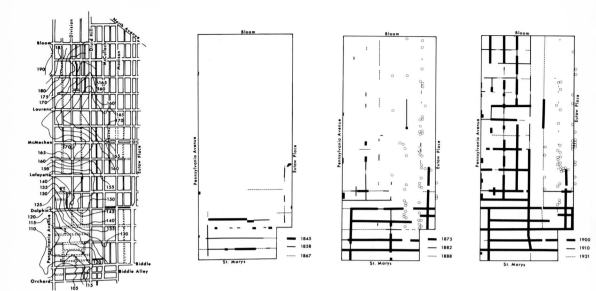

Figure 13. Racial mobility in the Pennsylvania-Eutaw corridor. The row-by-row extension of Negro occupancy has been traced by Raymond Snow and Andrew Frazier from City Directory listings. Movement outward from an 1833 nucleus in Biddle Alley to 1921 was complex, influenced by topography, commercial development along the road to Pennsylvania, and the width of the streets. Contour lines are shown at five foot intervals. Also shown (circles) are families listed in the Social Register in 1889 and again in 1921. They occupied elegant rows along Eutaw Place and Madison, the avenues which led to Druid Hill Park. Park squares in Eutaw Place were embellished in the 1870s and a fountain added in 1888. In the 1890s Eutaw Place was also the focus of the wealthiest Jewish families in the city. The high status families employed black servants, but twentieth century moves onto Druid Hill and McCulloch streets were a Negro middle class of school teachers and preachers. Pennsylvania Avenue became the scene of Easter parades, nighttime glamor, and famed Negro entertainers of the 1920s. Reconstruction has likewise proceeded along parallel axes. In the 1920s the Biddle Alley "lung block" (seven tuberculosis deaths a year) was demolished for school construction. By 1970 a pharmacy and another school, built over the avenue, replaced the heroin counter at Pennsylvania and Dolphin. New housing and a green network are planned further north, with Pennsylvania Avenue as the commercial and institutional backbone of "Upton." Along Eutaw Place, construction of the state office buildings was followed by consolidation of an institutional and commercial border for Bolton Hill and new garden apartments have been finished to the north. A steep social gradient still exists, from poverty on the west to upper middle class on the east.

stabilized Catholic immigrant neighborhoods almost as powerfully as sabbath restrictions produced compact neighborhoods of Orthodox Jews. The mixing of German, Polish, and Italian second generation is most evident in the suburban tracts. In these Catholic wedges one finds a wider range of variation in the proportions of immigrants of first and second generations. They add up to between 10 and 18 percent. Greek populations are often associated with Italian. There are also areas in which German stock populations are concentrated with-

out other Catholic groups present and some of these residents are German Lutherans.

Even very spotty ethnic "nuclei" such as the thousand or so Lumbee Indians from North Carolina appear to be developing an axis of outward hops and skips from the vicinity of Broadway and Fayette streets (East Baltimore) south to Brooklyn and thence to Glen Burnie in Anne Arundel County. The same path is followed by a sizable Appalachian population from western Maryland and West Virginia. People from South Baltimore along Light

Street tend to move to the same suburban areas.

Asians and "other Americans" (other than Canadian) are very recent immigrants, essentially the brain drain of the late 1960s favored by the change in immigration laws. They cluster around hospitals and universities. Asians are more strongly centralized than equally recent Caucasian immigrants and less centralized than black newcomers such as Jamaicans. Baltimore has a surprisingly small Spanish-speaking population. Cubans and Puerto Ricans have avoided Baltimore because in their search for jobs, education, and housing they are often treated as blacks. The Spanish-speaking people have not become established in distinct neighborhoods.

We have seen that people have been sorted by certain characteristics into wedge and ring distribution. This represents a certain amount of mobility within a context of apartheid. The ethnic variations are so elaborate that we cannot say who excludes whom: everybody excludes everybody else, except at the extremes —a wedge of white wealth and a core of black poverty. Income differentiation, while it is powerful in sorting at the neighborhood level, does not adequately explain the emergence of definite rings and wedges. A logic of producers and their dependents distinguishes the rings. In the next chapter, some classification of producer roles is proposed as a logic for ring and wedge.

The Tense Economy

At first glance the Baltimore economy looks very much like that of any metropolitan area in the nation, or a composite of them. It is not dominated by a single firm or line of production and has no pronounced image and no spectacular glamor sector. Overall growth rates are roughly in line with Baltimore's position as the nation's eleventh largest metropolitan area and fourth-ranking seaport and its location in Megalopolis. Its industrial and occupational structures, laid out in the census classes, are not unusual. They show little change, except for general trends in the national economy—more services are being produced and more clerical and professional workers are being employed. In its structural diversity the Baltimore economy is considered fairly well "buffered," and unlike Seattle or Detroit, it has not been especially hard hit by national ups and downs in the aircraft industry or oil prices.

But under the surface there is a great deal of turbulence. The Baltimore economy is an aggregate of highly specialized and differentiated activities, rather peculiarly knit together and undergoing complex changes. If we break down the production sectors to the right level of detail, we explode the apparent stability and discover the tensions, the vulnerabilities, and the sense of risk involved in its present growth strategies. Likewise, if we break down the occupational structure to the right level of detail by sex, age, and race, we discover a basis for the forms of social segregation and polarization described in the last chapter and get

some insights into current social changes and social tensions.

FIRST IMPRESSIONS

What does this factory town look like? A classic view from Federal Hill Park shows an immense foreground, the Inner Harbor, in various stages of total reconstruction. Looking east and north, through a forest of cranes in the ship repair yards, one sees a great gray-green sheet metal hulk steaming at water level —the chrome paint plant (Mutual Chemical), a visible example of the additions, accretions, and changes of 150 years' enterprise. Beyond, on the hill, sits the prestigious research and service enterprise, the Johns Hopkins Hospital, a clump of Victorian red brick turrets surrounded by assorted modern hunks of concrete, blind walls, air conditioning machinery, power house, and new parking tower. Farther east is Highlandtown, a hilltop covered with dingy glass and iron, the vast industrial cold frames of the 1920s. Off to the east a thin line of chimneys and a reddish haze mark the steel plant at Sparrows Point, its incredible scale, power, and din softened by seventeen miles distance. All of these industries show a tremendous resilience and vitality in their transformations. Each has reconstructed its techniques, its site, its markets, and its labor force, repeatedly building new values into its location.

To see the brand new industries, you have to travel out the expressway corridors or the beltway. Westinghouse and Western Electric plants built in the 1920s were the models for the modern low profile plant surrounded by vast parking lots and the sealed-off structures and brighter materials of the late sixties in the industrial parks at Timonium, Edison Highway, of the Baltimore-Washington corridor. The newer "dirty" operations such as the large chemical and fertilizer plants like Glidden or U.S. Gypsum, white with dust, have tended to concentrate in the outer reaches of the harbor, at Canton or Curtis Bay.

The basic geography of Baltimore industry is still the northeast-southwest axis, along the fall line or geologic contact of piedmont and coastal plain. Industry has spread out on the larger peninsulas and inlets of the coastal plain. This region has the advantages of tidewater shipping, ground water, relatively flat land, and a certain malleability. By filling and dredging, and by building piles, piers, and cribs, sites can be refitted and extended. The natural advantages have been reinforced by railroads and then highway construction, notably the Harbor Tunnel (1950s) and the North Point expressway (see Figure 4). The same geologic contact along the Atlantic coast is the basis for the commercial, industrial, and population growth of Megalopolis, which now reinforces the pull of this corridor for new distribution center and industrial sites.

THE LINKAGES OF GROWTH

We shall take three different angles for viewing the weblike growth of the economy and the ties between the private and public sectors. The first is the Baltimore-Washington corridor as a new industrial district. The second perspective is that of a large and specialized employer (Bethlehem Steel), linked into the regional economy. The third is an example of newly developed linkages within a diversified corporate structure (Easco). All have their geographical base in the coastal plain.

The Baltimore-Washington Corridor

New industrial sites in the corridor have grown by $5 and 10 million lumps on pockets of land. Piecemeal over fifteen years, public, private, and railroad initiatives have rebuilt the corridor and re-sorted the land values in a way that marries the old railroad access and the new highway access through spurs and feeders. Large amounts of land are devoted to railroad

car sorting and storage, truck terminals, and employee parking lots.

Corridor development is dominated by distribution operations and light or clean types of manufacture, oriented to product distribution rather than heavy raw materials or a large labor force. We find, for example, a GM parts depot for dealers in five states and distributors for foreign automotive enterprises—Volkswagen, Toyota, Mercedes, and Michelin. Marriott Hot Shoppes has a $9 million food-processing and distribution facility, while Macke employs 500 persons in a system for supplying food-vending machines. Carling's brewery (Canadian-owned) is one of six regional distribution centers in the U.S. After ten years of resistance, Baltimore's central produce markets have been relocated from the Inner Harbor to Jessup. Adjoining this site, Giant Foods has an automated warehouse with 4,800 gravity flow lanes and a central control console for picking off cartons of groceries.

Government services are a major growth sector in the corridor, as one might expect from the nearness of the federal capital and the state capital at Annapolis. The U.S. Department of Agriculture at Beltsville and the University of Maryland at College Park are a hundred years old and were jointly located, but they have expanded dramatically and independently in recent years. Both are large land users. So is the military base, Fort Meade. The new growth pole is the National Aeronautics and Space Administration. Its Goddard Space Flight Center cost $85 million to build over ten years and its Space Science Data Center near Greenbelt is newer and still more expensive. Of a thousand technical and professional personnel at Goddard, most have been recruited from out of state, and this has stimulated high value residential developments in Anne Arundel and Howard counties. Among NASA's important subcontractors in the region are the University of Maryland and the Johns Hopkins Applied Physics Laboratory in Howard County.

Another dramatic example of linkages between public and private enterprise in the corridor is in the vicinity of the Baltimore-Washington International Airport at Friendship. Three groups of developers acquired $1 million worth of land—about 180 acres—in three strategic strips, between 1966 and 1971. They have produced at least $50 million worth of development. The Sun Papers (April 5, 1972) traced the connections among numerous corporations, elected officials, and fund-raising politicians and thus documented a curious "complex," well known but rarely mentioned in textbooks of economic geography. In this complex we find a large motel and office buildings occupied by the National Security Agency and the state Board of Education and Department of Transportation. The Department of Transportation oversees the airport, interstate highways, motor vehicles, and port authority. Another large office group is the Greiner Company (Easco), private consulting engineers for airport expansion and state highway projects (see below). We also find among the owners and developers individuals tied to the airport limousine and taxi enterprise, state employees' and airport insurance contracts, the state liquor control board, the ownership of race tracks (state-regulated), and a pinball vending machine company.

Specialization

While a few resource industries are insignificant in Baltimore (leather, lumber, textile mill products), concentrations of most manufacturing sectors are in line with national averages. Proportionate to its labor force, Baltimore has its share of the nation's employment in food and apparel industries, printing and publishing, furniture making, paper, plastics, chemicals, fabricated metals, and electrical equipment. But if we break these sectors down into more detail there are decided differences. The location quotient for the subsector steel blast furnaces is five or six times the national average. Shipbuilding is three times the national average, while "other" transportation equipment is merely average. And shipbuilding is concentrated primarily in two firms—Maryland Drydock and Bethlehem—one of which is the major steel supplier as well. In electrical equipment, the bulk is produced by a few firms—Western Electric and Black & Decker, the region's largest locally owned firm, maker of home power tools. A large firm which appears diversified may be quite specialized, such as the Koppers Company (Pittsburgh) which has 3,350 jobs in the Baltimore region. Its five local plants produce an impressive variety of items—power transmission couplings, electrostatic precipitators, cooling fans, corrugated box machinery—but in fact half the operation is the production of piston rings and seals for diesel engines.

Bethlehem Steel, with a payroll of over $300 million, is a kingpin in the interlocking structure of the regional economy. Its linkages cut across private and public sectors. Its local sales include inputs to the other big export-base firms such as GM, Western Electric, and GE. Located near Bethlehem for convenient supply are Thompson Wire, Anchor Fence, and Ray-Met, a firm which supplies steel pile and does custom construction in an international market. A Venetian blind maker takes a million dollar's worth of steel each year. Bethlehem supplied the steel to a local bridge manufacturer for the state's new parallel Bay Bridge. Bethlehem interests are believed to have weighed heavily in the choice of technology for the regional mass transit system. The company's ship repair yards are essential to the local port and its shipbuilding division recently launched a new class of giant tankers. Their production thus directly and indirectly influences exports from the Baltimore region.

Bethlehem's investment program over the last ten years included $60 million for a new ore pier and channel to accommodate ore supercarriers and a still bigger investment in basic oxygen furnaces. They make steel in forty minutes, where the older open hearth furnaces took four to nine hours. These technological changes are closely related to another $28 million investment in special equipment for making light flat-rolled products such as chrome-coated can steel for the city's long-established can-making, food-processing, and brewing industries.

As part of an international complex with its main offices in Bethlehem, Pennsylvania, Bethlehem Steel is characteristic of a whole class of enterprises whose ownership and top management are outside the region. Of *Fortune's* 500, only two have their home offices in Baltimore (Easco and Black & Decker), while dozens have only branch plants. Baltimore businessmen complain of a "branch plant mentality." Baltimoreans tend to own shares in industries located elsewhere, while outsiders own the industries located in Baltimore. The ultimate threat is, of course, closing out of a branch plant and all its employment, as happened recently in the brass and copper industry (two century old firms) and the rayon mills (Mount Vernon-Woodberry). As Bethlehem's Sparrows Point plant is profitable and large new investments have been made, it sends no shivers down local spines. But there are other side effects of outside management. Some firms are resented for their reluctance to invest in local cultural and image-building activities. Baltimore's position in international banking is weakened because national corporations handle international documents and foreign exchange through their corporate headquarters and their New York bankers.

Diversification

The new thrust of industry is corporate diversification. A large number of manufacturers have adopted the strategy of diversifying into service and real estate activities and then scattering their risks in the metropolitan area or still more broadly. For example, the McCormick Company, a century old Baltimore spice dealer and food processor, created Maryland Properties, Inc., which developed Pulaski Industrial Park on the east side, Security Industrial Park on the west side, and in the north, at Shawan Road, Hunt Valley Inn, Golf Course, and Industrial Park. The inn has become the favorite executive club of the northern wedge, and there are nearly 10,000 employees in the industrial park.

The remarkable global expansion of multiproduct corporations like ITT have their modest counterparts in the Baltimore economy. Easco is one of the two Baltimore-based corporations in *Fortune's* 500. Developed by acquisitions and mergers, several of its operating groups are headquartered in Baltimore. The most important one locally is J.E. Greiner, an engineering firm intimately connected with Maryland state highway projects for seventy-five years—in particular the Chesapeake Bay Bridge, the new "parallel" bridge (next to it), and the Interstate system in Baltimore City. Its recent thrust is in engineering and environmental impact studies.

The Arundel Corporation also grew by successive mergers of firms in dredging, sand and gravel, shipbuilding, ballast, and sanitary disposal. As their quarries were depleted and their land fills finished (from dredging work), they owned 8,500 acres, all in large parcels on prime highway access in the industrial corridor. Their ventures, evolving too fast to describe in full, suggest the kinds of corporate linkages which are emerging as the basis for a metropolitan-scale economy of rising land values. Arundel traded 722 acres in Howard County to the Rouse Company for development of Appliance Park, where GE will employ 10,000, adjacent to Rouse's Columbia, designed as a "new town." Arundel owns the 350 acre quarry site for the Cold Spring "new town in town" project for 12,000 residents. Arundel is developing a large industrial park at Linthieum and a 414 acre Arundel waterfront at Fairfield (opposite Fort McHenry) is widely discussed as a site for a large scale amusement and tourist center. Nationally Arundel has participated in huge joint construction ventures on the Snake River and water tunnels for Manhattan and Los Angeles.

When Henry Knott, one of the state's largest builders, acquired an interest in both Easco and Arundel, he effectively integrated these enterprises. Their growth is founded on the capture of sites and environments privileged in the total growth process of the metropolitan area. The complex and ultramodern corporate structure is built upon a remarkable continuity of family strategies over two generations and on a tough web of informal social (Irish and German Catholic) and political connections.

THE LABOR FORCE

Flux in the techniques of production, sites, product lines, and corporate structures all imply adaptations for the labor force. Extreme specialization and rapid technological change mean that within the region there can exist at the same time shortages of skills, skilled immigration (as of doctors from India and the Philippines), unemployment among the highly skilled (physicists and engineers), obsolescence of older skilled workers, and unemployment or underemployment of less skilled persons and new high school graduates.

Not only are there changes in the job market—the supply and demand for various skills—but there are important changes within the region in the *locus* of job, residence, and journey to work. If we divide the entire urban work force into five classes of jobs and look at where they live, each class proves to be segregated from the others to some degree and each has a unique geographical pattern (see Figures 14 and 15). Even this crude division reveals the relationships between people's residential situations and their roles in the economy.

The "primary" activities—mining and agriculture—are not discussed at length, as they include only 1 percent of the work force, and only 5 to 8 percent even along the northern "rural" border of the region in Carroll and Harford counties. More important (15 percent) are the "secondary" occupations—that is, manufacturing workers: skilled crafts, semi-skilled or factory operatives, and self-employed craftsmen. Most of them work in factories or workshops and handle materials, tools, and machines. The "tertiary" occupations include a great variety of service jobs—food service, cleaning service, security or "protective" personnel, nontechnical hospital workers, and personal services. They may work for an industry, an office, a government, or a retail establishment. The less familiar term "quarternary" workers applies to those (28 percent) who do routine information processing—such as clerks, typists, key punchers, programmers, and bank tellers. Most of them work in offices. "Quinary" workers also process information, but in nonroutine ways. They include professional and technical jobs, many management jobs, nurses, and teachers.

RESIDENTIAL PATTERNS OF THE LABOR FORCE

The most highly segregated category is the quinary. Although 21 percent of the work force is in this set of occupations, most tracts have a much larger or a much smaller percentage of their residents in such jobs. In a few tracts, quinary occupations are numerous and dominant; they account for 30 to 55 percent of the labor force. These tracts occupy a surprising share of the metropolitan area, as this class consumes a great deal of land. They occupy the green wedge north from Baltimore City into Baltimore County, a second southwest wedge (nearly all of Howard County), and three sizable areas south in Anne Arundel County. A map of quinary jobholders corresponds quite accurately to maps of high income, high homeownership, high home value, low density, and a high proportion of detached dwellings. The absence of quinary workers from certain districts is also striking. A large core area in Baltimore City has less than 10 percent in quinary occupations. In many tracts they are as rare as 2 percent.

Service jobs (tertiary) map out almost a mirror image of the quinary jobs. The city core, outside the central business district, has most service workers. Concentrations over

50 percent are chiefly the black ghetto neighborhoods. There are also sizable parts of Anne Arundel County over 40 percent and a narrow westward corridor through Carroll County.

These two groups of occupations are the most unlike in status and pay and in composition by race and sex (Figure 16). Their opposition suggests the way in which the polarization of residential space is built into the division of labor in the metropolitan economy. They represent the extremes—a highly specialized, highly educated and mobile elite work force, and a proletariat of service workers whose mobility—social and geographical—is relatively limited. Mobility of the quinary work force is evident, for example, in the concentration of brain drain immigrants of the 1960s from Europe, Asia, and Latin America into certain census tracts around research and educational institutions and hospitals and the concentration of highly technical and professional personnel from other parts of the United States around the NASA installations.

Quinary jobs can be regarded as decision-making occupations. These workers have a strong grip on decisionmaking within their highly specialized sectors of industry, technology, and government. They have a strong influence on the decision frameworks or range of choice of other sectors, through their role in the "quinary industries" such as banking and insurance, education, research and development. Moreover, when we relate this to the lifestyle of their residential districts, we see that they are decisionmakers in all domains of life. That is, they have a higher density of choice in their personal lives—the management of a house and real estate and a budget with credit options. Because they have automobiles, they have a farther range of decision, not only in choosing, trading, and financing the car, but in the daily choices of routes, shops, etc., and an extra degree of freedom in searching for another job or home. Accumulated experience in their education and career development has increased their mobility, their information network, and their flexibility in relating their personal decisions to opportunities and changes in the economy and the environment. People in this sector do not always see themselves as having an adequate range of choice or power of decision because they are limited to extremely specialized and narrow sectors in their work. Many

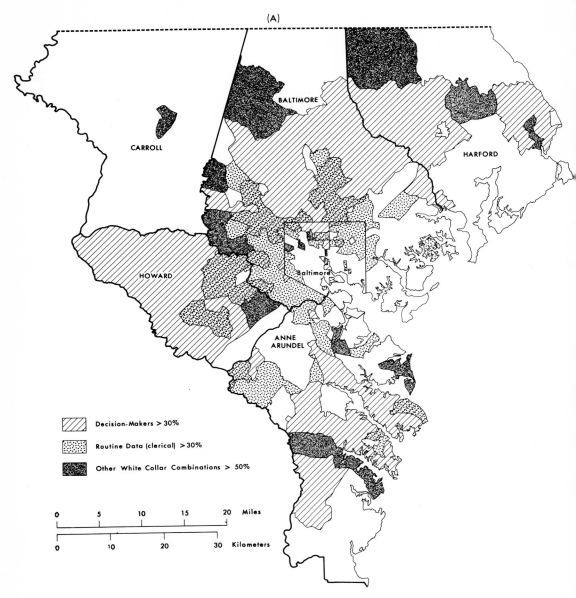

Figure 14. White collar (A) and blue collar workers (B) at home. (A) Residential patterns of decisionmakers (nonroutine handlers of data) and clerical workers (routine handlers of data) resemble the map of new, high value, resident-owned housing. (B) Manufacturing workers are concentrated in the industrial coastal plain corridor, while service workers are concentrated in the core region of public dependency.

work exceptionally long hours, but they have some ability to negotiate their work schedules, holidays, and vacation seasons. They appear to have characteristic maladies of tension, heart disease, use of alcohol, or tranquilizers. The need for mobility and flexibility places great stress on the small family social unit.

In contrast, the core area where there are few quinary jobs is a nondecision zone. There is no room to maneuver. One rarely knows a

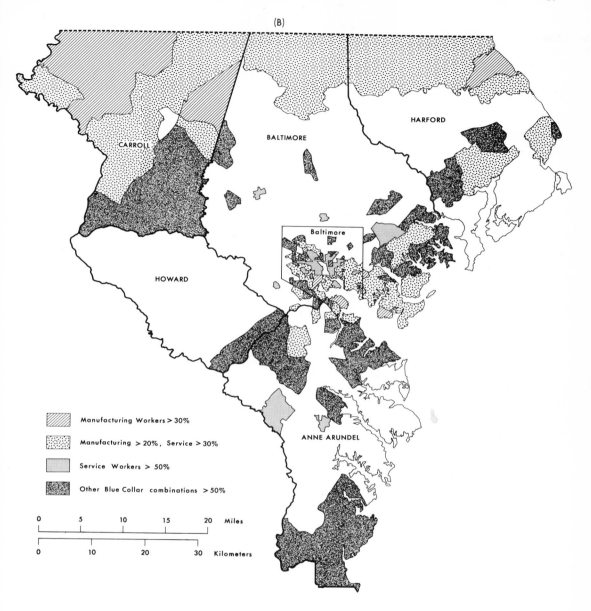

(B)

Manufacturing Workers > 30%

Manufacturing > 20%, Service > 30%

Service Workers > 50%

Other Blue Collar combinations > 50%

CARROLL

BALTIMORE

HARFORD

HOWARD

Baltimore

ANNE ARUNDEL

0 5 10 15 20 Miles

0 10 20 30 Kilometers

person whose job "changes" things. A large share of service workers have dirty jobs, night shifts, or variable schedules which they cannot manipulate. In daily life, residents are at the mercy of rigid bus routes and the weekly rent book. They have no financial flexibility and because income is smaller the range of shopping choices is more constrained. These workers have, on the average, much smaller household spaces to organize, maintain, or personalize and much smaller public spaces to supplement them. Personal spaces are more frequently invaded—theft, fire, noise, odor—and there is a corresponding sense of lack of control of neighborhood—invasion by outside traffic and manipulation by absentee owners and business-men. In addition to health problems directly associated with crowding and space (for example pedestrian accidents and respiratory diseases), some health problems appear to be

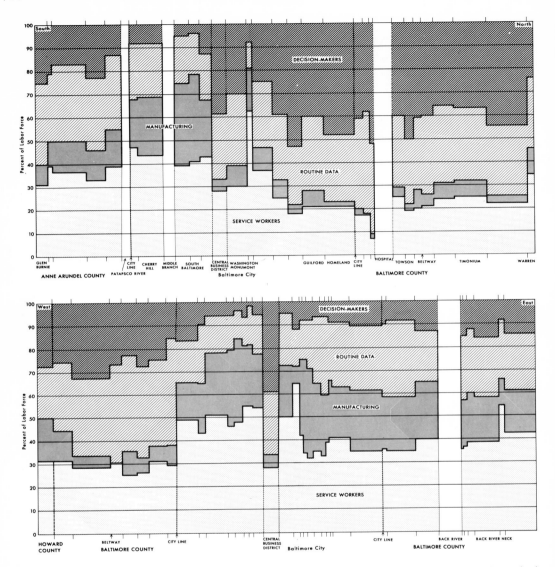

Figure 15. Labor force stratigraphy. The two cross sections, east-west and north-south through the center of town (Charles Center), show both a ring and a wedge effect. Blue collar workers (service and manufacturing) ring the central business district, but more so in the east and south.

associated with the constraints of "nondecision"—possibly the incidence of personal violence, use of hard drugs, and the common "ghetto headache."

Manufacturing workers have a degree of segregation comparable to the quinary workers, but they are not found in the same residential areas. There is more overlap between service workers and manufacturing workers than be-

tween manufacturing workers and either of the other groups. Together manufacturing and service can be regarded as "blue collar jobs," but manufacturing workers are generally unionized and better paid.

Quaternary workers (clerical) tend to share the geographical spaces of quinary workers. Both are "white collar" jobs, regarded as clean and "nonmanual." Quaternary and quinary

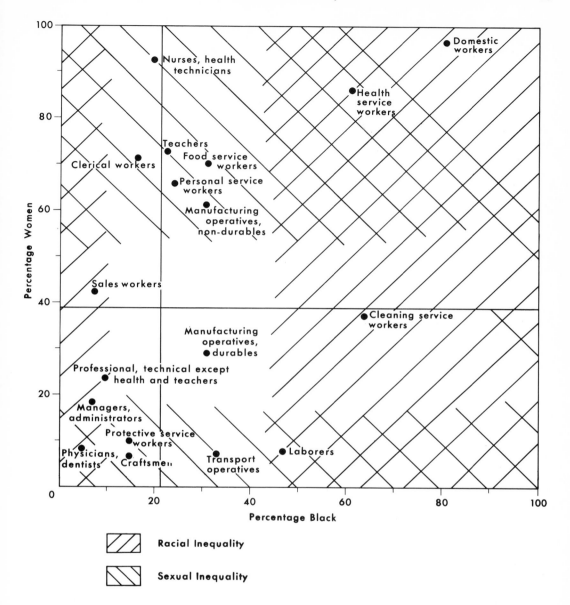

Figure 16. Metropolitan Labor Force by Race, Sex, and Occupation. Only one job category falls within the nondiscriminatory region around the "normal" percentages of blacks and women we might expect from their rates of participation in the region's total labor force. Occupations are ranked to approximate national norms of median wage and prestige. The ranking is crude because of race and sex differentials within each job category. The wide wage spread, from a median of $20,000 (1) to $1,700 (18), depends on maintaining race and sex wage gaps and a differentation of job types as shown. The three indicators of status thus tend to be mutually reinforcing. The wide spread of income provides mechanisms as well as "justifications" for segregations in housing, on the job, and in education.

workers share work space in office buildings. A large number are concentrated in the central business district. In production structures their jobs are often matched—the manager has his secretary and file clerk, the doctor his receptionist. In such cases, quaternary workers are more often women. The residential pattern of quaternary workers is a wide circle on both sides of the city-county boundary. The band does not extend across the coastal plain zone. An extension toward the northwest matches the wedge of Jewish settlement, with exceptionally low levels of manufacturing employment. The white collar aspirations of the Jewish community are well documented in the Associated Jewish Charities study—60 percent of men between twenty-five and forty-four are in professional or executive jobs, 12 percent in sales. Of the older generation, fewer are professionals and executives, more are in sales and proprietors of small business. Of the employed women half hold clerical jobs, and teachers are the next largest group.

A geographer is tempted to note that factory workers are living on the coastal plain, while the quinary and quaternary workers— white collar—are located chiefly on the piedmont (see Figure 15). It is not a simple matter of geology and soils, but a complex piece of history. Geographical spaces have been appropriated as social spaces.

PRODUCTION SPACE AS SOCIAL SPACE

The main concentrations of industrial workers are neighborhoods of old industry which formed distinctive local economic bases, often associated with a particular social base or ethnic mix. A simultaneous wave of immigration and industrial growth allowed a particular social group to develop or capture an economic base and a neighborhood. This process was repeated again and again. New production systems underlay new systems of social relations. Changes in the production system repeatedly disintegrated these local social systems and opened the way for reorganizations in the local social geography. Dozens of historical examples of these processes can be found—shipbuilding on Fell's Point, oyster packing in Canton, can making in Highlandtown, the cotton mills at Woodberry, the sweatshops of Old Town, dock work on Locust Point, railroad shops

at Mount Clare, the aircraft industry at Aero Acres. . . . We shall choose a set of complementary types of production systems from among the largest and most modern enterprises in the region. We shall see that production spaces are social spaces. Differences in production roles mesh with the social "distances" between classes and ethnic groups.

As we might expect from its size, Bethlehem Steel plays a role in the structure of a large series of social spaces (Figure 17). It has an elaborate internal society, as it employs 34,000—18 percent of all employed in manufacturing in the region. The company trend is typical of the overall economy: the number of production workers is not growing as fast as the number of technical, managerial, clerical, and service and transport workers, who are now one-third of their work force.

There were elaborate lines of seniority in the 217 shop units. Transfers from one shop to another implied loss of seniority and determined the worker's place in the line for further raises, promotions, training programs, or layoffs. Over several years federal and state civil rights commissions and the Office of Federal Contract Compliance pressured the company and the union (United Steelworkers of America) to modify the rigid framework of social space in the plant, on the grounds that the company's 8,000 black workers (one-quarter) were frozen into low-paying jobs. Environmentally, they occupied the hot spots, near the open hearth furnaces and away from the air conditioning, and filled the dirty and dangerous jobs like acid cleaning in the coke ovens. The limited compromises of 1971 involved unit mergers and reduction of tests for some hundreds of job classes.

Here again, Bethlehem was merely typical of the way in which the social spaces of production units were structured. In 1970 at the advanced materials works of Armco Steel in Baltimore, blacks were also more than a quarter of the production force, but no black had ever participated in the foreman training program, only one of ninety-nine plant supervisors was black, only one of 152 white collar management level employees, six of 216 clerical workers, and five of 198 professional, technical, and sales employees.

The Social Security Administration is a massive "white collar factory." Like the blue collar factories, it provides a local neighbor-

Figure 17. Sparrows Point steel plant. Bethlehem Steel Corporation's Sparrow's Point steel plant, one of the largest in the nation, occupies about 2,100 acres just southeast of Baltimore on the Patapsco River near Chesapeake Bay. The plant turns out a variety of steel products such as plates, pipe, reinforcing bars, wire rods, wire, nails and staples, wire strand, sheets, blackplate, and tinplate. Alongside the plant, at the left of the photo, is Bethlehem's Sparrows Point shipyard, one of the major builders of tankers and cargo vessels in the United States. Bethlehem Steel photo.

hood-building social and economic base. As the national records and data-processing center for the nation, Social Security employs more than 16,000 persons, 80 to 90 percent of them women. The majority are in the lowest four civil service grades, such as keypunch operators who are new high school graduates. This office alone would account for a third of the growth in the female clerical sector in the last decade, or 7 percent of all the quaternary jobs now in the region. The equal opportunity effort in federal jobs in the 1960s made this an economic base open to black women, as the post office had once been for men. The black community is now funneling large numbers of young women into the quaternary sector. The mechanism for a shift from the blue collar factory to the white

collar factory lies in the educational inputs and the black community like the Jewish community utilized the public schools and insisted on education for girls. The public schools have been most effective in fostering occupational success in the quaternary sector, as they teach routine processing of information and reward personal adaptation to the regimented, authoritarian, sedentary, and sanitary environment of the white collar factory.

Social Security has occupied various buildings in downtown Baltimore since it began in 1936, but its largest modern installation is at Route 40 West and Security Boulevard (Figure 18). Like Bethlehem on the east side, the white collar factory has generated a complex community space on the west side—row hous-

Figure 18. Social Security complex, 1973. Photo by Maps, Incorporated.

ing, apartments, and shopping centers. Its hiring practices have contributed to opening a thin wedge of black residential settlement in Baltimore County. Anxiety over that emerging wedge contributed to the decision that the further expansion of Social Security will take place at a center city renewal site.

Another white collar factory, the Chesapeak and Potomac Telephone Company (AT&T), appears to have a rigidity of social spaces complementary to those found at Bethlehem, Armco, and Social Security. C&P has some 14,000 employees in Maryland (not all in the Baltimore region). 1971 testimony to the FCC stated that only seventy of 2,000 managers were black. The segregation of shops and wage levels depended on a geographical structure for the various operating divisions. Most of the black women employees were operators

at inner city exchanges. There were no black personal secretaries, communications representatives, or engineering assistants at the downtown headquarters until recently, but blacks filled all the mailroom jobs. Blacks filled most jobs in the printing and typography operations in East Baltimore, but very few of the jobs in the central accounting office at Cockeysville, to the north.

SHIFTS IN THE DIVISION OF LABOR

It is apparent that the character of the four occupational groups is related to the elaborate segregation of production by race and sex (Table 1). By means of a more detailed classification of occupations, Figure 16 shows how strong these patterns of division of labor by race and sex are. Baltimore differs from other

Table 1. Occupational Groups by Race and Sex, Metropolitan Area, 1970

| | Percent of People in Each Type of Job | | | | | | |
Type of Job	Total Women	Total Blacks	WM	WF	BM	BF	All Workers
Decisionmaking jobs	27	10	68	22	5	5	100
Routine data handling	64	14	31	55	5	10	100*
Manufacturing workers	33	33	44	22	23	10	100*
Service workers	28	29	55	16	17	12	100
All workers	38	22	50	29	12	10	100*

*Figures do not add to 100 because of rounding.
Source: Census of 1970

metropolitan areas only in having a larger share of black workers.

Over the last ten years, changes in the composition of jobs and jobholders have shifted the percentages but have not changed the underlying structure of occupational roles assigned by race and sex. One hundred and seventy-five thousand new jobs were added to the labor force, largely in services and public sectors. As more women entered the labor force, they were absorbed into sectors traditionally reserved for women—nurses and teachers among professionals, clerical (about half), and health and food services. Many of the new jobs were at minimum wage. The only improvement in the wage structure was the disappearance of domestic household help. A slight shift from racist to sexist domination of jobs was not especially favorable to the black community in view of their high proportion of women wage earners.

The critical fact which reinforces this system is that we have not a mere *division* of labor, but a *hierarchy,* in which women are paid less than men, and blacks are paid less than whites. Limited alternatives in the job market create a different balance of supply and demand, which depresses wages in certain sectors. Interactions of "racism" and "sexism" produce an infinite number of options for playing off the interests of one group against another, with the result that Baltimore industrial interests in their economic development literature point to the unusually low family budget of Baltimore factory workers, low differential pay for shift work, and a lower rate of unionization.

Structural changes in the labor market are naturally reflected in labor organization. The growth of service and professional jobs and relative stagnation of factory labor have shifted labor-management conflict into the arena of public and service enterprise. But the job competition of various social groups has favored conflict *within* the unions. Effective unionization of new sectors has thus been limited by the social conflicts built into the division of labor. Three-quarters of manufacturing workers are unionized in the region, but a much smaller share of other workers. Baltimore has exceptionally large nonunion sectors in construction and trucking. Few women workers and black workers are unionized except in the clothing industry. A major breakthrough on all those fronts was organization of hospital service workers (Local 1199E). City teachers, policemen, and hospital workers became militant in 1974, but without significant gains. In the last few years most racially segregated locals have merged, but they maintained the seniority and preferential interests of the larger white membership (as at Bethlehem and in dock labor and construction). The city's black firemen formed the Vulcan Association to exercise a voice in the white-dominated firemen's union.

Over the next ten years, the sense of competition among groups for jobs can be expected to continue as a source of tensions, because of the changing proportions of various groups in the labor force. In this sense, conflict is structural in a competitive economy. The Regional Planning Council projects that the younger generation (twenty-five to forty-four) will increase from 40 percent (1970) to 50 percent of the labor force. Although the black work force will remain constant overall (one-quarter), in this age group it will nearly double. There are also more women among the younger workers. We may expect to see acute competition for low wage entry-level jobs, a struggle between younger and older generations for managerial and policy roles, and further pressures for early retirement and technological obsolescence of older workers. Because of the way demographic structure and labor force structure interact, all these forms of competition are likely to be expressed in the familiar rhetoric of race and sex.

THE REGION'S SOCIAL SPACE

The metropolitan region is a single area in terms of its economic structure. There are small differences among the counties in terms of the economic sectors for which people work. But in the actual occupational categories there are decided differences: city residents include half the factory workers of the metropolitan area, nearly half the service workers, but only 41 percent of the routine processors of information, and only 32 percent of the decisionmakers.

Geographically, the total growth of the metropolitan area requires a massive centrifugal movement of capital—capital formation, disinvestment or transfer from the central city, and investment on the new fringe. The development of residential spaces is only one aspect of this. In many ways movements of "human capital" resemble movements of fixed capital. The highly capitalized population—that is, quinary workers—has decentralized fastest and exerts immense pull on capital in the retail sector. We now find supermarkets and bank branches located in a suburban ring pattern. They have disappeared from a large inner city ring.

But this centrifugal movement does not imply a trend toward an equilibrium. The growth employment locations are cut off from public transport and the present dispersion of industrial operations is unfavorable to economical mass transit. Therefore, access to new jobs is reduced for the young, the less skilled, the lower paid, and married women in one car families. Even if no direct race discrimination were operating, the effects are discriminatory because blacks are overrepresented in all these categories and in their central residential location. In other words, the present setup in the language of development economists is a "low level trap." Occupational exclusion and residential exclusion reinforce each other and this

tendency is becoming more severe as industrial growth moves into Carroll and Howard counties.

Meanwhile, the technical growth of the economy produces at once demands for specialization, capitalization, and flexibility. The problem for the worker is much the same as the problem for the industry—he must invest more time and resources in his (or his children's) education, choose and concentrate on a narrower specialty. Yet he sees that these investments are subject to great risks of obsolescence and he has to preserve what flexibility he can.

At the level of neighborhood and social group, these processes continually produce disintegration and recoalescence. Neighborhoods appear to go through cycles of vitality and flight in which the movements of capital (mortgage money and public investments) run parallel with the movements of human capital —the young and educated households.

Because of the changing job mix and the changing labor force composition, old patterns of division of labor by sex, age, and ethnic group must break down. But traditions of racism, sexism, and paternalism provide a framework for venting frustration, hostility, and anxiety in the face of the personal threats of technical and economic change the individual cannot control. This context of structural conflict is the basis for the polarization of the region into spaces of control—home turf and places of threat.

At every scale in this local geopolitics—household, neighborhood, county—one discovers strategies of defense. In the suburban ring each household stakes a claim, creating a private hedge against inflation or a private speculation and defending it through local zoning restrictions. Older inner neighborhoods defend their investments, social identity, and status aspirations by struggling to keep the parochial school alive, retain the football stadium, or find enough young Italian couples to keep Little Italy alive as a restaurant district. In the very core, individuals buy guns or fierce dogs or they band together to fight off a new liquor license or to demand a community-controlled school. Many defense strategies have been cast at the scale of the metropolis—the city-suburban ring—because this is the basic political frontier between a zone of sunk capital and a zone of capital investment. Other struggles have been restructured into a geopolitical struggle at this scale, a level where public investments are made.

In other words, the Baltimore economy not only produces steel for the North Atlantic community and electric drills for the nation, distributes cars and groceries to six states, and fries chicken for Baltimoreans, but as a by-product it produces Baltimore society—the class structures of consumption and the geographical structures of distribution. It produces in some measure a "Baltimore person," with a sense of competition and vulnerability, and an awareness of the limits on his ability to control his own personal life.

Development and Redevelopment

The breakdown of old vital spaces and reconstruction of new vital spaces, as described for certain industrial districts, is an example of a more general process. Just as the vital space of the Susquehannock and Piscataway Indians was constrained, then broken up, destroyed, and reconstituted into an agricultural or planter economy, most of the agricultural space in the metropolitan area has in turn been constrained and broken up. It is now rapidly being reconstituted into suburban fabric. Some parts of the area have gone through further cycles of redevelopment which we recognize by the massive clearance of structures. Others are renewed by a more continuous and less obvious process, like the metabolism of the human body—the simultaneous breakdown and reconstitution of tissues.

We shall focus on the role of public enterprise in several different kinds of redevelopment—the port, the downtown, the inner city, and a series of speculative transformations of successive rings out to the fringe of conversion of agricultural land. These transformations, which seem like local phenomena and functionally distinct operations, are actually part of a single growth process. The metropolitan area is a whole and its physical transformation is only one facet of this process, a surface we can see. A second facet—the movements of people—can be traced with more difficulty. The third facet is an invisible movement of capital. We have to consider the total renewal process as this triple transformation.

THE PORT: PERENNIAL RENEWAL

Since 1730, the port of Baltimore has been recognized as the real urban potential, the growth frontier of the Maryland economy, and the squall line of competition with other cities. The port has grown, like the city, outward from its original all-purpose piers in the Inner Harbor (several times redeveloped), to a forty-two mile crocheted edging whose pattern can best be seen from a boat or plane (Figure 19).

But to maintain its competitive characteristics and accommodate the ever larger vessels in international trade requires ever greater investments in dredging—deepening and maintaining channels and anchorages. This trend was already evident 150 years ago, when Baltimore began asking for federal subsidy to maintain its sixteen-foot channel to Fell's Point. The current effort is to complete and widen the fifty-foot deep Chesapeake Bay channels and to improve the seventeen mile Chesapeake and Delaware sea level ship canal. The C & D Canal is a $100 million project; it is being deepened from twenty-five feet to thirty-five and widened for two way twenty-four hour operation.

In the economic geometry of ports, Baltimore's location has the characteristic trade-off of advantages and disadvantages of an inland type of port. It is relatively distant by sea from the major ports of northern Europe. Vessels must travel 150 miles (a twelve hour

Figure 19. Baltimore Harbor, 1973. Photo by Maps, Incorporated.

run) up the Chesapeake Bay from Norfolk (Hampton Roads), or come through the C & D Canal. But the port of Baltimore is fifty to 150 miles closer than any other U.S. port to midwestern markets. In terms of cost structure, 150 miles ocean distance is short, while 150 miles overland is long, and rail freight structures tend to favor Baltimore. But to capitalize on the advantages of such a location requires also ever greater investment in overland transport systems.

The original Inner Harbor piers and warehousing were privately developed by merchants. In the next stage the entrepreneurs were charter corporations. The Canton Company built railroad belt and switching lines. It has extensive piers, warehousing, a new ore pier, and a new industrial park, and has expanded into industrial realty and freight traffic management beyond the region. Ironically, the Canton Com-

pany, owned by the International Mining Company of New York, is also port management consultant to the rival port of New Orleans. The B & O Railroad developed in succession the Locust Point coal piers, grain elevators, the European immigrant pier, and port facilities at Fairfield. In the early 1900s the city and the Western Maryland Railroad jointly developed the south side of the point. During World War II outlying specialized port installations were extended by heavy industries (See Figure 19).

But as the need for redevelopment emerged, the private corporations proved sluggish. In part this is an overall decline in the innovative capacity and financial health of railroads, but there are other reasons: they are interested in rather limited types of captive freight—the coal and grain traffic not subject to truck competition. B & O land is privileged: it is no longer locally owned, but by its early charter it does not pay the local property taxes which would force its redevelopment into income-producing property.

These conditions—the need for major capital, redevelopment, and effective total port management—led to creation of the Maryland Port Authority in 1956. The MPA's first ten year $67 million investment plan has turned into a twenty year $200 million plan, and the MPA is expected to unveil a still bigger program looking to the 1990s. The evolution of this plan gives insights into renewal strategies in the face of risk. The initial project was the creation of Dundalk Marine Terminal, with a new core-type pier, where ships tie up at marginal berths, in contrast to the older finger piers. This kind of mooring allows more flexible use of the total length of pier for ships of all sizes, and more flexible use of the back-up land area. Baltimore has become the most important port in the nation for importing foreign cars. Specialized rail yards and trucking facilities have been built to handle the inland hauls. A $20 million project for filling an entire cove at Hawkins Point is destined for automobile handling.

The dramatic change came in the container race. In 1955, at Bethlehem's repair shipyard, McLean Industries had the first ships converted for carrying trailer truck bodies. Their operating subsidiary, Sea-Land, created a container-handling port on a site leased from the Canton Company. Container shipping of general cargo reduces dock labor radically and makes loading and unloading faster, saving time in port for the ship. An hour's work for twenty men is turned into a ten-minute job for a small crane crew. It also means faster door-to-door delivery, less handling, significantly less damage and theft. The swift turnaround of capital is the basic strategy. By 1972 Sea-Land had ordered new fast ships built in Europe. Each will carry 1,100 containers and the Sea-Land fleet alone will have enough space to supply the projected North Atlantic commerce. They expect to go to a feeder or shuttle system, unloading at a few points and sending containers in smaller older ships to smaller ports. Baltimore has already been downgraded in this service by Sea-Land. The port of Greater New York is number one, but Baltimore is investing in new container-handling facilities in a race with Hampton Roads, Philadelphia, and New Orleans. The Dundalk Marine Terminal site has been expanded by 200 acres ($18 million) for six new container piers, and on Locust Point the MPA has exchanged land with the B & O, United Fruit, and the Western Maryland Railway for another massive container facility.

A related development is the "ro-ro" or roll-on roll-off ship. The whole truck—tractor and trailer—goes on the ship. The MPA is planning a $6 million ro-ro terminal on the south side of Locust Point. Martin Marietta's LASH system is a variant of this—lightering containers from large vessels onto barges and from barge to dockside supercargo plane. Their concept of intermodal access is calculated to recycle a thousand acres at Chesapeake Park into an industrial park. Originally an aviation enterprise, they have their own complete airport-seaport on Middle River, northeast of Baltimore.

It is evident that competition of the shipping corporations occurs at the national and international scale, in a climate of swift technological change. Large variations occur in bulk cargo movements, too. Grain exports, for example, were cut into by the Saint Lawrence Seaway opening to Chicago (1959) and by federally subsidized Mississippi River improvements favorable to New Orleans. The grain handlers union has declined since from 600 to sixty-five men. Baltimore interests complain that the grain elevators and handling facilities controlled by out-of-state interests are not being modernized to remain competitive.

The overall trend in the seaport, as in manufacturing, is toward heavier capitalization and specialization of facilities. It is essential to maintain flexibility in the use of land and facilities. The intense competition among East Coast ports and among interests within the port of Baltimore appears to stimulate overbuilding and high risk. Port management is therefore a tightrope act, in which state and federal governments are expected to perform, picking up the lumpiest and most risky investments. The same public initiative and risk-bearing are relied on for redevelopment of "over sixty-five" industrial spaces, such as the Camden station area and Highlandtown; the city recently agreed to redevelop half of Fort Holsbird (federal) as an industrial park.

DOWNTOWN RENEWAL

Baltimore's downtown experienced a forced renewal from a great fire in 1904 which leveled the financial district and the wholesaling and dock perimeter. It was immediately rebuilt, but very modest changes of plan were introduced—a few street widenings and a rearrangement of the docks. By 1960 the whole downtown was ready for retirement. It was physically obsolete, financially stagnant, and psychologically demoralized. Baltimore began to feel economic competition with other cities changing their skylines and fiscal competition with its own ring of suburbs. This produced a do-or-die sense of crisis among certain financial interests, including department store owners. They formed the Greater Baltimore Committee, which hired planners and in 1962 unveiled its

Charles Center plan to the mayor and the public.

This plan is a remarkable example of a strategy for change. (Atlanta is probably the other example of such a strategy.) A single large project—Charles Center—was calculated to generate a dynamic sequence (Figure 20). Like the port development plan, but more explicitly, it would lock in on ever larger investments and transformations. The strategy worked and most of the projected bigger efforts are now well underway. The criticism one can make is that it has proved hard to diverge from this strategy or from the interests and strategic control which this group

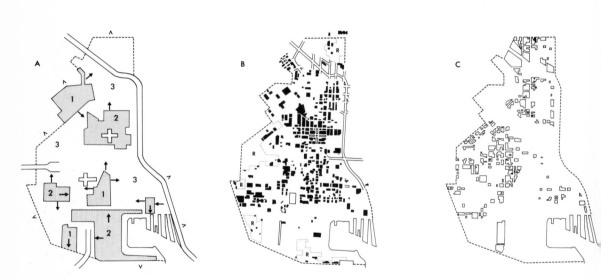

Figure 20. Strategy and tactics of downtown redevelopment. "As a nation we are deeply committed to an ethic of growth and development. . . . This growth mentality is a fundamental element of our economic system and a tremendous amount of money flow and rewards of the system are dependent on and involve physical growth. A city's physical growth is symbolic of the fight for life against death." (A) "The State Office Complex, Camden Industrial Park, and Charles Center acted as Phase I tactical moves. The Inner Harbor, University of Maryland, and Mt. Vernon plans (Phase 2) took advantage of the climate set by Phase 1 and began to exert counterpressures, as new places 'where the action is'. . . . The next set of moves will take advantage of previous tactics with new action thrusts, for example, the Community College, retail mall and the expected response of the private market as Phase 3. . . ." (B) Hard Structures: Shown response of the historical or visual importance, and new or bulky buildings and engineering structures. " 'Hard' means those buildings with stable, intensive uses. They are expected to remain indefinitely, and can generate new developments around them." Residential areas are also shown (R) but not defined as hard or soft. (C) Soft Structures: A matrix for action. " 'Soft' means those older buildings with high vacancy rates, and low assessments. . . . It is to the City's advantage to achieve the most aggregate total space and activity in Metro Center. It can do this by guiding new development into areas of generally smaller and older buildings." Source: Regional Planning Council and Baltimore City Planning Department, *Metro Center*, 1970.

represents. Large financial resources have been taken from federal urban renewal monies, but the strategy was conceived before these were available. With the reduction of federal funds, the city is still committed to very large investments.

Charles Center, an office building project, cleared thirty-three acres (Figure 21). It is elegant and modern and includes attractive and rather successful public outdoor spaces, yet the scale is very much a home place. A visitor alighting from the airport limousine finds himself in a human scale environment, a perfect introduction. The project was situated to promote future connections or extensions around the edges—west by the "Lexington Mall" toward Baltimore's wonderfully ugly retail shopping district on Howard Street, east down the hill toward the government offices and courthouse district, which is forever refurbishing its monumental character; southeast toward the finan-

cial district, originally the homes and counting houses of the shipping merchants.

The original Charles Center strategy would boost employment in the central business district, despite a small residential population. This implied more commuter movement, so the Charles Center included a maze of underground parking garages and created strong pressures for additional large public investments in expressways to serve commuters from the white collar districts on the north and west. A rail mass transit plan was redesigned as a star radiating from Charles Center, an expression of its overriding objectives as a downtown commuter and downtown shopper system.

Downtown renewal has to be considered incomplete. The retail position has continued to deteriorate, the convention role has not materialized, and Charles Center is ordinarily a dead space at night. Recognition of these faults has been built into larger projects and the re-

Figure 21. Charles Center, City Fair, 1973. Baltimore City Department of Housing and Community Development.

newal operation has been a learning process, as well as a pilot project for a much bigger venture on the south, the Inner Harbor, which is expected to increase its annual property tax yield tenfold. Successful features of the Charles Center as a planning operation were retained for the Inner Harbor project. The organizational structure—Charles Center-Inner Harbor Management, Inc.—is a nonprofit corporate subsidiary of the city's Department of Housing. A policy of strong architectural controls and design competitions has been continued. Mies van der Rohe designed One Charles Center, Pietro Belluschi the IBM building, Louis Kahn the Constellation Place Hotel. The objectives were to restore a residential population and a nightlife in the core. Staging has been calculated to prove its workability to the skeptics—first a nursing home and apartments for the elderly, then an entertainment complex, Science Center (Museum), a large hotel and restaurants, then high income apartments with waterfront views.

Meanwhile, a grand model and grand strategy known as Metro Center have evolved extending the downtown renewal to a much larger core and emphasizing the kinds of highly specialized activities which can be expected to grow as the metropolitan area grows. Into this strategic framework have been grafted a new campus for the Community College of Baltimore, a new federal courthouse and offices, and the state's World Trade Center. Still debated is a costly stadium and convention center. The original federal downtown renewal investments were intended as public pump-priming to stimulate private investments, such as the new buildings of U.S. Fidelity and Guarantee Company, IBM, and C & P Telephone Company. However, as in the port, one might infer that public and private investments have in fact primed the pump for much larger subsequent public investments.

The major gamble and the ultimate future for private investment appear to be high income downtown living. Shopping renewal hinges on this purchasing power. The attraction of private capital into these schemes requires the speculation incentive of the mass transit stations. But the residential strategy also requires a critical mass, endangered by competition among large projects and lifestyle alternatives in the Inner Harbor West, Cold Spring, and high-rise centers in suburban and exurban loca-

tions such as Towson, Columbia, and Lake Linganoke. All of these have been threatened with financial collapse in the "stagflation" of 1973-1975.

For redevelopment, the Metro Center plan conceives of the city as a mass of physical structures which are either hard or soft—that is, more or less susceptible to being remodeled (Figure 20). It illustrates the renewal process as an investment strategy, striking, as Churchhill said (referring to a larger geopolitical stage), at the soft underbelly.

SLUM CLEARANCE

The first push for massive clearance of old residential areas occurred in the mid-1930s. Before federal low income housing programs or renewal subsidies took shape, Baltimore leadership staked out a belt of blight for clearance. During World War II the tactical program was housing for war workers, recast in 1947 as federally subsidized slum clearance and public housing, then as "urban renewal." We should also consider as slum clearance massive programs of expressway construction and inner-city school replacement.

There are three basic ideas behind all these forms of slum clearance. The first was a strategy of protecting a downtown. Clearing a ring of blight was a corollary of the downtown redevelopment strategy. This was already evident in the Emmart report of 1934. Concepts of a downtown labor force, downtown shopping, downtown image, and downtown security were connected to ideas of what land uses, populations, and purchasing power should be engineered in the surrounding belt. Expressway access tied in with this strategy.

The second goal always proposed is renewal of the city's tax basis. The return on public investments would come in the form of a future stream of annual property taxes. This is not a powerful argument for residential renewal itself, but when tied in with downtown renewal it pays off.

The third goal is a public health goal. Baltimore always attempted small slum clearance projects after great epidemics. In 1816 Ruxton Lane, the cholera lane, was demolished. A century later at the time of a polio epidemic, a strip along St. Paul Place was demolished for a monumental, beautifully landscaped park. In 1925 the "lung block" was torn down for a school. More recent demolitions include the flophouses on Pratt Street, the "Block" (a honky-tonk and vice district on east Baltimore Street), and the heroin corner on Pennsylvania Avenue. The conviction is irrepressible that deteriorated housing, deficient plumbing, and crowding into small dwelling spaces contributes to the spread of contagious diseases and perhaps to other threats such as crime, delinquency, drug addiction, illegitimacy, and mental illness. The presence of such pathologies always defined a soft underbelly for clearance and redevelopment, regardless of the new land uses proposed.

All these goals converged to make the black community the target. Relocation in postwar renewal projects has run 80 to 95 percent black. The prime obstacle to this overall program of physical and fiscal renewal has, from the first, been the massive displacement of people involved and the particular problem of people too poor to offer a profitable market for new private enterprise housing. In residential urban renewal, Baltimore has been a leader in the nation, and has exerted pressure for larger federal subsidies in public housing. The renewal program has been a politicized learning process over forty years. We can look at the process and ask what are the results.

Certain goals have been achieved. Baltimore has recycled more housing and more residential land than most cities of its size in the country and is continuing to demolish its pre–Civil War neighborhoods. There are now scarcely any dwelling units in the city without toilet and bath; central heating is swiftly becoming universal, overcrowding is radically reduced, and the population is generally better housed. Tuberculosis is declining and infant survival has improved. But the strategy and mechanisms by which this has been achieved have had dramatic side effects in the recycling of people. The number of households displaced by public actions (renewal, expressways, and school building) between 1951 and 1971 was at least 25,000 (75,000 people, see Figure 22). It is a small percentage of all the moves in the metropolitan area, but because of the concentration of actions in small spaces, short periods of time, and selected populations, the effects are intense. Between 80 and 90 percent of those relocated have been black, at least two-thirds renters, perhaps one-fifth single individuals. Most were relocated within the city. Government carried

out nearly all these operations. The rate of displacement accelerated over the period, from about 600 households a year in the 1950s, to 800 in the early sixties, to 2,600 in the late 1960s. In 1970 the city housing department had over 8,000 open cases for residential relocation.

THE CITY'S HOUSING STRATEGIES

The original public housing concept, modified to meet war worker housing needs in 1940, involved clearance of five to ten acre sites and construction of several hundred new low cost units, densely laid out, in two and three story rows. The wartime move ins were magnificently staged affairs, but it was impossible to replace the entire population on these sites. The scale of the relocation problems generated two kinds of experiments. The first was low cost housing on isolated fringe sites. This was reasonably adaptive during war time expansion of factory jobs, job training, and mass transit to work from these areas. But they have suffered since from the containment of manufacturing jobs, distance from the center, and the decline of public transit. All the projects were segregated by race. The white projects have proved viable as cooperatives or rental (Armisted Gardens, Aero Acres), but the black projects (Turner and Cherry Hill), located to insure maximum isolation, have suffered more from pollution problems and a lack of local shopping and institutional services.

The other experiment was rehabilitation of dwellings. Known as "the Baltimore Plan," the first effort (1952), in East Baltimore, became a code enforcement model for federal rehabilitation subsidy programs. It has since generated demand for more ambitious redevelopment in the same area. The second effort was Harlem Park (West Baltimore), where alley dwellings were demolished and inner block parks were designed with the participation of block clubs.

In the national architectural and financial context, the Baltimore Housing Authority moved in 1953 toward the construction of high-rises on cleared sites in two major clumps, east and west. They occupy whole tracts and fill whole elementary schools (Figure 22). Urban renewal projects were also extended over forty, fifty, or seventy acres, in order to coordinate design of schools, parks, fire stations,

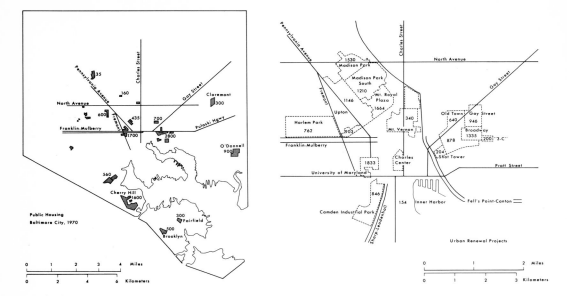

Figure 22. Units of public housing (left) and households displaced by urban renewal and public housing (right), Baltimore City, 1951–1971. Figures do not include displacement of the 1960s for highways, although the corridors are shown. The zones of massive displacement along Gay Street and Pennsylvania Avenue axes are now built up with large concentrations of public housing. Redevelopment lags generally ranged from three to thirteen years.

stores, and to get more flexibility in the rearrangement of the site. Nevertheless, difficulties of scheduling such large operations led to a housing gap in the mid-1960s. Massive relocations from the expressway coincided with renewal clearance. At the same time the city began to experience the environmental defects of high-rises, and the public housing waiting lists were filled with hard-to-relocate people. It became obvious to every one (it had always been obvious to the black community) that urban renewal meant black removal. The implications were laid bare and there was a crystallization of resistance—black resistance to removal, resistance of adjoining communities to a relocation spillover threat, and resistance of neighborhoods to construction of new projects.

The uproar resulted in a reorganization of municipal agencies, new stress on rehabilitation, fuller citizen participation, and smaller projects, including public reclamation and leasing of isolated vacant houses. The most popular new program is "homesteading": several hundred families are rebuilding abandoned "dollar homes"—in Stirling Street for example—with the help of municipal loans and technical assistance. By sharing contractors, designs, ma-

terials, and the crises of financial bureaucracy, their "barn raising" has restored social solidarity as well as physical environments at the scale of the block. Urban renewal has come to be seen as a therapeutic process rather than a grand scheme that would some day be complete. In this sense it began to look like the port or the downtown—redevelopment in ever-widening circles. The Community Renewal Program has the entire residential area of the city scheduled for differing degrees of remodeling, renovation, or conservation.

The city now has 15,000 public housing units. Yet its initiative and leverage in the metropolitan housing market is small and does not allow it to keep up with its ambitious rate of "slum clearance." There are another 2,000 "low rent" and 4,000 "moderate rent" dwellings, privately built and managed but federally subsidized. Social rigidity has been built into the various projects in terms of income and age segregations, which produces financial vulnerability for the public housing authority and for the households living in the projects. The projects are no longer officially segregated by race, but their location and use as a relocation resource favors de facto segregation. Of public housing occupants, 89 percent are black. Managers must tread a fine line. Because they must select people in greatest need, not served by federal home mortgage or private markets, two-thirds are dependent on public assistance. Only 9 percent are adult men, including some in their seventies. By federal policy, rents must cover management and maintenance costs, but the tenant's rent may not be more than a quarter of his income. This squeeze produces an intense concentration of households in a narrow income range. It also produces a narrow margin for management in responding to changes in fuel costs, or the need to replace refrigerators and roofs as whole projects reach a critical age. Baltimore's Housing Authority has been one of the most successful managements in the country, still solvent, and maintaining standards for maintenance, security, and tenant stability.

THE SUBURBAN FRONTIER

The energies of private enterprise, having largely abandoned the city, are being poured into the urbanization of the surrounding five county area. The fundamental geographic structure was already in place by 1960. The industrial advantages of large portions of the coastal plain were developed during World War II and affirmed by generous industrial zoning. The beltway and major radials of the interstate highway system were built or under construction. Suburban housing development had overflowed the beltway in the sixties on the southwest, north and northeast. But the rolling terrain and geologic variety of the vast semicircle of countryside north and west of U.S. 1, and a number of unspoiled necks and rivers (peninsulas and tidewater inlets) offered exceptionally attractive opportunities for further suburban development. Baltimore probably has more potential in this respect than any other metropolitan area in the country. The differentiated and fragmented character of the land is fundamental to the way in which development is taking place. As in nineteenth century Baltimore, the natural differentiation seems to lend itself to community building at a scale compatible with builders' economics—several hundred to a thousand dwellings—and with the buyers' conception of an exclusive neighborhood. The landscapes of central Maryland, more than most regions of the U.S., offer immense opportunities for the environmental and recreational lifestyles developers are now designing for high income people. At Lake Linganore, for example, west

of New Market, Brosius Homes built seven dams on a 4,200 acre site; one, a prize winner, has a water slide, lagoon, and fountain at the base. Its supernatural boulders were moved into place with machinery. (Its financial structure was less elegant, and the builder has since filed for bankruptcy.)

As Figure 23 shows, the basic ring of new single family developments is a zone in which half the households moved in within five years (1965 to 1970). It is beyond the beltway, and particularly strong just over the border of Harford County, deep into Howard County around Ellicott City and Columbia, and in Anne Arundel County along the Magothy and Severn rivers toward Annapolis. By 1971 Anne Arundel County was the leading area for single family dwellings. These new developments feature streams, private lakes or marinas, woods, and pasture for horses. The names hint at the premium combination of prestige and outdoorsiness, recalling the Maryland plantations, the hunts, and the English aristocracy—Fox Meadows, Camelot, Quiet Inheritance, Tanager Forest. Apartment developments, including garden and rental townhouses, are a more recent phenomenon and they are concentrated along the major radials at the beltway and beyond (Figure 26).

Beyond the construction zone, land is being held and transferred for speculation and future construction. In 1972 nearly 4,000 acres of land in Baltimore County (perhaps 6,000 acres in the region) were being taxed at a lower farmland assessment, although the land was already subdivided and zoned for business, industry, or multifamily. Anne Arundel County retains an unzoned category for areas not yet open to development. Harford and Howard counties retain lot requirements of three, five, ten, or even twenty acres for the same purpose, but Baltimore County recently removed its restriction. The object of the "nonzoning" tactic is to encourage orderly development instead of sprawl, but it also boosts land prices in the zones open for development and stimulates a race to capture and manipulate the future zoning of areas not yet open.

SUBURBAN DEVELOPMENT STRATEGIES

As the frontier moved out and population grew—26 percent in Baltimore County over the sixties, 44 percent in Anne Arundel, 50 in Har-

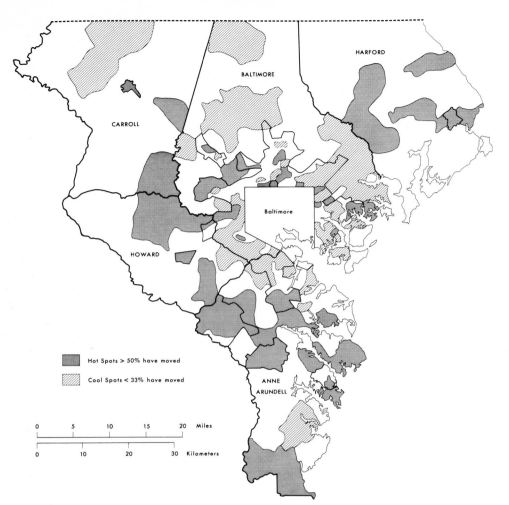

Figure 23. Residential turnover outside the city. This measure of turnover captures only one five year time frame in a moving picture. Suburban hot spots are zones of new construction. Many lie outside the sewered area. Beyond the line less than half the dwellings are connected to public sewers. The suburban cool ring is a zone of development of the ten years before 1965. The residents are staying put, paying the mortgage, and probably—if they are outside the line—having trouble with their septic tank system or their neighbor's.

ford, 77 in Howard—intense competition was focused on the large sites close to the junctions of beltway and radial expressways. These high access points were the obvious locations for industry, offices, shopping centers, and high-rise high density residence. There were immense rewards for the capture of these special locations at the right moment. But a sense of timing as well as spacing was essential to capture the right combination of buying price, interest rates, and leasing opportunities. They were the object of geopolitical strategies—to achieve coordination in space and synchronization in time of public zoning actions.

The principal public forum for development issues has been zoning hearings. In 1968 Baltimore County reworked its entire zoning classification and maps and introduced a "cycle system" for considering rezoning petitions seasonally, to allow analysis and hearings focusing on one geographic sector at a time. In the 1970 cycle there were requests to rezone 2,000 acres in this county. The larger and more controversial sites have new value primarily because of government initiative. For example, a joint venture was proposed for the site adjoining a mass transit terminus planned near Owings Mills. County planners wanted to concentrate development into the beltway ring, into corridors already well served with water and sewers, and into high density *sector centers*. But this strategy added value to already appreciating nodal sites such as Towson, Reisterstown, Eastpoint, and Whitemarsh. For example, one developer requested rezoning for 500 acres in a proposed sector center at Kennedy Expressway and Whitemarsh Boulevard for a vast shopping district, motel, office park, and golf course. (He owns 900 acres more just across the expressway.) These conflicts produced a political crisis in Baltimore County. Thousands of citizens came to the hearings and expressed particular rage at the behind-the-scenes behavior of the county council men and a handful of well-connected zoning lawyers. All seven county councilmen are elected at large and the one most closely connected with developer interests apparently has never carried his own district.

SUBURBAN SOCIAL STRATEGY

Aside from the battle for "upzoning" of high value nodes, the other source of zoning controversy in Baltimore County involved protective "downzoning" of several of its twenty small black communities. It was probably a minor episode in their destiny, but reveals the underlying powerful agreement within the county on social strategy. The effort of several county planners to provide information to local communities and the public resulted in their being fired by the county executive. Evidence for the mechanisms by which a lily white Baltimore County was being created was brought out in hearings before the U.S. Commission on Civil Rights in August 1970. First, these small century old communities are isolated. In Edgemere, Turner, and Pines, the street networks do not connect with adjoining white communities except via the single main street. In other words, the positive factors that differentiate and reinforce neighborhoods also reinforce segregation by race; black neighborhoods are isolated from white neighborhoods. Their small size insures a weak voice in local politics and makes possible the discrimination of public services. Small "colored schools" were operated at least until 1954. The county did not pave the streets and has not extended sewer and water lines to several of these communities, even where adjoining white communities are served. The residential pockets are kept at a rural level of services, while surrounding areas were brought to suburban standards.

Zoning was part of the strategy (Figure 24). Half the black communities in Baltimore County were zoned for industrial or commercial use. The environmental implications are obvious— the tankfarm, the sewage treatment plant, the quarry noise, the junkyard as neighbors. But more serious, the community cannot grow. It can be liquidated. Turner (near Dundalk Marine Terminal) offers this scenario: Several hundred apartments were built with federal money for war workers at Bethlehem Steel. In 1954 the management (the Baltimore City Housing Authority) tore down a third and sold off the rest to a private owner. In 1966 the owner tore these down, evicting 1,330 people who still lived in them, and redeveloped the land for industry. Fifty white-occupied homes on the same side of the tracks were not included in the industrial zone. In other cases, black communities were torn down to provide suburban amenities for others. More than fifty homes were demolished for Towson Junior High School, the county police and fire station, a new road, and a power substation. No relocation opportunities were made available. Many families had to move into Baltimore City, and the black population of Towson has declined by half. The remaining East Towson and Lutherville communities have been under threat for several years from a ring road. Expressways in the eastern part of the county are scheduled to wipe out Bengies and bisect Edgemere, and three freeways will reinforce the isolation of Turner.

The several discriminatory mechanisms are mutually reinforcing. Why perpetuate a residential community without sanitary facilities? But why extend sewers to an isolated community of a hundred homes when it is destined for industrial redevelopment? In the wake of the 1970 civil rights hearings, several communities (Chase-Bengies) obtained downzoning to residential status and East Towson resi-

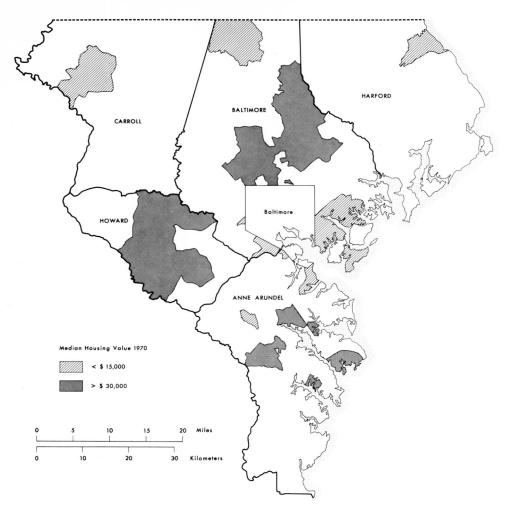

Figure 24. Median value of resident-owned homes, 1970. High value homes are found in the high income wedge to the north, a western wedge, and southern clusters of new white collar development. Lower value homes reveal an industrial belt of working class homeowners with a rather consistent mix of housing from the 1940s, 1950s, and early 1960s.

dents were promised some relocation in the county. But this is only the tip of an iceberg. These public debates over the survival of a few hundred homes reflected a broader policy, whose more important feature was keeping blacks out of new areas. The black population of Baltimore County increased by only 4,500 people in the 1960s, its white population by 124,000. The percentage black remained fixed at 3.5. Black families occupy less than 2 percent of owner-occupied homes in the county. Yet the black population of the city increased 30 percent. In the metro-

politan area they are nearly one-fourth of the population and the black middle class made income gains and could afford homes in the county. We can only infer some forces of resistance in Baltimore County.

How do these barriers work? As in other neighborhoods the front lines of defense are the real estate and financial institutions. Federal mortgage insurance was widely used by developers arranging homeowner financing, but it declined in the suburban area after 1962 when President Kennedy ordered the FHA to become colorblind. A Maryland fair housing law was passed about the same time as a federal fair housing law (1968), but enforcement is limited. The "steering" practices of at least one large realtor are now subject to continuous statistical evaluation, to insure his compliance with the law.

Baltimore County government is the third line of defense. The county council and voters have consistently refused to participate in federal programs of public housing, urban renewal, relocation assistance, or creation of a county "workable plan." Anxiety about these federal programs often comes to the surface.

The case is more complex in Anne Arundel County, with 12 percent black residents. Blacks are represented in school and city jobs, but not significantly in the police force. A quarter are concentrated in the ghetto fourth ward in Annapolis, but many others live in contained settlements. Isolation and limited services are common here, too, but they also occur in a number of white communities. Black families own 6 percent of the owner-occupied housing and 3 percent of the newly built homes of the 1960s.

The new town of Columbia in Howard county was the first serious and successful effort in the region to produce a new and stable integrated residential community of a large size. Population is believed to be 13 percent black and is not localized. This was possible thanks to the personal determination of the developer, James Rouse, the total community control in his hands, and the high income mix. Class selectivity reduced anxiety over racial integration. The location was ideal for federal civil servants and professionals already committed to and accustomed to integrated work environments. However, Columbia ran into financial trouble, and Rouse has not succeeded to the same degree in achieving a wider range of incomes and occupations.

As the Civil Rights Commission commented, "While protecting their own interests, suburban areas are legislating for the entire region." By 1970 there was no new single family housing being developed in the city and job development was also taking place primarily in the counties.

IN BETWEEN

As the fringe is built and the center is rebuilt all the in-between rings are being transformed

Some examples will show how the chain reaction occurs. Each link represents a shift of capital.

Clearance and relocation from central renewal operations produced strong impact on adjoining neighborhoods and certain corridors of "soft" urban tissue. Half to three-quarters of the people from a demolition area relocate within a mile. This effect observed in Baltimore resembles the diffusion models familiar to geographers or models of osmosis in body chemistry. The process is dramatic because of its swiftness. In the area south of Druid Hill Park, over two or three years, population increased 20 percent within the same set of three story houses. Elementary school population doubled, rent for a three room apartment increased, and rental income per house increased more. The same process was important along the Park Heights corridor (northwest), and along Greenmount Avenue, Patterson Park Avenue, and Washington Street. Windfall profits did not last long; they depended on permissive zoning and lagging code enforcement (Figure 25). The profitable phase was followed by progressive deterioration, high vacancy rates, depreciation of market values and assessments, and abandonment of the houses. An owner of 1,000 rental properties in this ring was tried in housing court for code violations on 200 properties. He was in federal prison at the time and claimed he could not make repairs because the federal government had frozen all his assets to recover $10 million in income taxes.

There seems to have been a rapid movement of capital into new construction and very little into maintenance and renovation. This is true in both the public sector (schools and city office space) and the private sector and has been favored by federal grant mechanisms and income tax rules. For example, the rule permitting deductions for depreciation of property over ten years favors nonmaintenance and resale or abandonment at the end of ten years. Abandonment of houses in Baltimore reached a thousand per year. This is not nearly as high as some cities, but is particularly serious in a row house city. Relocated households express intense frustration at seeing "slum" conditions of disinvestment and crowding follow them as they move.

Meanwhile, in the next ring out, racial turnover has occurred (see Figure 12). Conditions

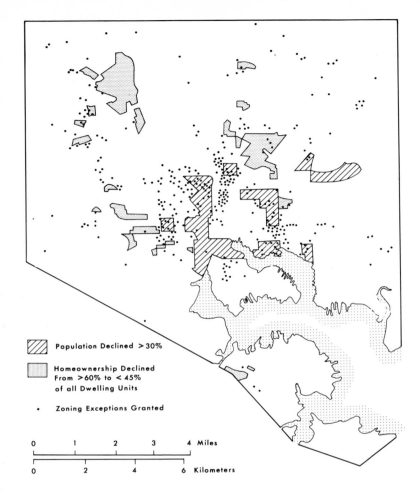

Figure 25. Rings of residential change in the city, 1960 to 1970. The ring of population decline over 30 percent (shaded) is associated with urban renewal clearance. Surrounding this is a spillover ring indicated by zoning exceptions granted (dots) for conversion of houses to multifamily dwellings, two to six in a house. Additional conversions occurred within zoning norms. Home ownership declined sharply in the outlined tracts, from at least 60 to below 45 percent of all dwelling units. The transformation of homeowner to renter in this third ring is associated with racial turnover and expressway impact, as in Rosemont. Sources: Harvey et al., 1972, and 1970 census.

"ripe" for block busting often include a sizable population of elderly homeowners and weak market demand by whites because young families are attracted to new suburban alternatives. The classic mechanism of the 1960s was documented by the Activists, Inc., from real estate records. In the Edmondson Village area (census tract 16–8) 94 percent of the 1970 households had moved in since 1960. Nine hundred houses changed hands, many of them twice, in 1962, 1963, and 1964. A single speculator, operating thirty real estate corporations, bought and resold a

third of the houses (half the transactions). The price to white sellers averaged $7,419, to black buyers $11,418. The speculator took the difference, as well as financing charges. The financial institutions were crucial to the operation. The three largest commercial banks in Baltimore provided him with working capital, $3.5 million in personal loans on three to six month terms. He arranged mortgages for his buyers from a savings and loan company. In most cases, he retained a second mortgage; later he had the transaction refinanced through the loan company. (Twenty-four other savings and loan associations in Maryland had also become captives of such speculators in the sixties.) When the FHA began offering loan guarantees in this area, 260 more sales were financed at an average price to buyer and seller of $9,357 and the speculator's operations were dramatically reduced. The FHA has, in the 1970s, replaced the speculator as the chief financial agent for neighborhood racial turnover, through its 221(d)(2) program in the city (See Chatterjee, Harvey, and Klugman).

In such turnover areas, the schools were quickly overcrowded, as younger families replaced older ones. A perceived decline in the quality of the school (crowding and low teacher morale) reinforced household decisions and hastened "white flight." The swiftness has to be ascribed to racism in the total housing market, availability of new housing for white families on the suburban frontier, and demolition of housing of less affluent and black households on the central renewal frontier. The squeeze hastened turnover in the middle ring, as blacks would pay higher rents than whites. Not only were black households squeezed financially, but they were frustrated by the feeling that, despite their financial sacrifice (higher labor force participation), the "ghetto" was following them. Some of these neighborhoods are very attractive, and feature beautiful gardens, as in Edmondson Village, Northwood, and Forest Park. They vary in income level, but in each case community effort to maintain racial integration has met tough obstacles. It became very difficult to obtain "respectable" mortgage money in the zone of turnover and maintenance investment on rental property was radically reduced, even while large sums were mobilized for investment and mortgage finance in the suburban fringe.

As documented by Harvey and Chatterjee, the partitioning of the housing market into submarkets, each with its own financial institutions and clienteles, has promoted over the entire market higher levels of indebtedness for housing, higher interest rates, and higher profits of developers and financial intermediaries.

Other curious opportunities have appeared in the metropolitan growth process. Each transformation requires a flow of capital and a scramble to capture the windfall of change, concentrated at particular locations. An example is the meteoric rise to wealth of wrecking contractors chosen to benefit from the city's demolition work. Another is the creation of a new chain of parking lots on vacant city-owned renewal lots, private lots "ripening" next door to them, and garages in the inner harbor renewal district. The expansion of the parking business has allowed a cluster of black entrepreneurs to enter urban capital formation. Somewhat on Ianni's model of Sicilian immigrant families who moved in a generation from illegitimate to respectable businesses, this group has developed from a springboard of "sportsmen's" activities (numbers) to politics, parking, real estate, construction, food processing, and supermarketing.

The growth strategy of city and county depends on capturing private capital. Despite state and federal revenue sharing, Baltimore City receives half its revenue from the local property tax. But to attract private investment, governments must invest heavily in organizing and equipping public spaces and income opportunities for private enterprise. The entire operation is a pyramid or chain letter in both the public budget and private real estate. Since the net movement of capital for urban construction is outward, Baltimore County or Howard County can be highly selective of industry, commercial projects, and homebuilders. The present political jurisdictions are structured for city-suburb opposition and they pursue different strategies of public investment. It is important to recognize that their different strategies are economically and politically rational. As in the labor market, conflict is structural. In this context, race discrimination and inequalities of income are played off against each other, reinforcing the very structure of inequality.

Mobility and Uncertainty

A civil rights commissioner asked a Baltimore County public works engineer in 1970:

> Might priorities for these projected roads be re-ordered if federal support for such roads weren't forthcoming?
> Yes, that is conceivable because, really, the top priorities for roads are to use up all the federal money we can. Certain roads qualify for federal aid where others will not, so it has been our aim to use up the federal funds wherever possible. (U.S. C.C.R., Transcript, p. 101)

Transportation investments are the biggest chunks of public urban capital. In transportation the most intensive, longest range, and most costly urban planning has been done. Current estimates for the construction of Baltimore's twenty-five mile expressway system and the first phase of a twenty-eight mile mass transit system are over $3 billion (1973). Even port development does not approach this. It is roughly the total real estate tax basis existing in Baltimore City. Each of these two schemes is described as a delicate and well-conceived system which cannot be tinkered with or modified. Nevertheless, the program has been changing for over thirty years and is still the focus of controversy and uncertainty. It is impossible to tell the full story of expressways in Baltimore in a few pages. I will simply try to sketch the dimensions of the two programs, emphasizing the ways in which they are connected and the way they bear on the problem of uncertainty.

Creating a beltway, like a lasso around the developed core, was not difficult, since it created new real estate values and opportunities at every exit and relocation problems were minimal. Likewise, it was not hard to build the Jones Falls valley expressway south toward town, although it took more leadership. State funds were voted in 1951, and once Congress created the Highway Trust Fund (1956) for federal subsidy, beltway construction moved fast (1961 and 1962). Its last link, the Outer Harbor crossing, is under construction. State Roads Commission projects for highways like spokes out from the beltway were also located without serious obstacle. But the program met resistance in the connections through the developed core.

The city had made plans as early as 1942 for an "east-west" highway to handle through traffic and the Franklin-Mulberry corridor was the first area in which the uncertainty was concentrated and over which it has hung ever since. This West Baltimore ghetto was the "soft underbelly." The corridor was bought up by a couple of land companies and gradually became derelict. The period of public acquisition and relocation—the tenants were mostly black and mostly poor—was in the mid-1960s—twenty to twenty-five years after the original plan was made.

Likewise, a firm plan was announced in 1956 for an expressway through Rosemont and Leakin Park. No further investments were made in the development of the park. The formal condemnation lines were fixed by ordi-

nance in 1966, ten years after the threat. Rosemont was a community of middle-aged middle
class black homeowners. The coincidence in
1966 of relocation of several thousand people
from Franklin-Mulberry with the "taking" of
homes in Rosemont provoked strong resistance.
Neither group had reasonable relocation opportunities or adequate replacement values
for their housing. Beyond the actual "take"
strips, both communities were severed and
homes were cut off from services and con-
veniences. There had already been many up-
roarious highway hearings, exposés, and
confrontations, but the new resistance to black
removal was a more serious threat because it
resonated with nationwide vibrations. The
mayor and the Interstate Highway Division
responded with a new tactic. They contracted
(1967) for a new, impressive planning instru-
ment to match the magnitude and challenge
of the problem. Known as the Urban Design
Concept Team, it was a $5 million consultant
team which incorporated engineering and
architectural firms, landscape planners, and
young specially hired "people-oriented" planners. Their task was

> to integrate the road by means of its form,
> scale and materials into both the man-made
> fabric and natural topography of the city
> ... from the point of view of the driver,
> and from the point of view of the city
> dweller—objective was to bring these two
> views into harmony, to maximize the bene-
> fits to both.

The planning venture, applauded nationwide, was nevertheless under rigid constraints.
The team was ordered not to deviate from the
set of designated routes. Its paying client, the
Interstate Highway Division, was an ambiguous
structure composed of engineers and appointees
of both city and state, committed to spending
federal money (90 percent). Politicians and
construction interests were eager to insure the
local injection of federal funds.

The still simmering Rosemont resistance to
acquisition was aired in three nights of hearings
(August 1968) in front of professional flak
catchers from the Interstate Division. The
politicians did not attend and enraged citizens
of twenty-four disparate organizations oppos-
ing the expressway formed a coalition known
as MAD—the Movement Against Destruction.

The Design Concept Team, deeply split, recommended one deviation from the original route—
to avoid Rosemont by going through a cemetery. The condemnation line was lifted early in
1971. Rosemont had been condemned for fifteen years in principle and for five years in law.
During its "uncertainty" it had lost its solid
homeowner character and become rundown.
The city was holding 500 houses. Since then,
$10 million has been earmarked for rehabilita-
tion of the neighborhood to counteract the
effects. It is a striking example of the fact that
a city cannot live without a future and that
parts of the city were sacrificed—deprived of
their future and therefore of all investment—in
the debate over the future of a "greater Baltimore."

ENVIRONMENT AND EXPRESSWAY

Baltimore's expressway struggle followed the
major themes of American national life, and
in 1971 the rhetoric of civil rights was replaced
with the rhetoric of environmental concern.
Resistance jumped from one neighborhood to
another and different organizations in MAD
took turns carrying the ball. Although the Concept Team has been dissolved, their environmental recommendations provide a guide to
still unresolved conflicts. Their ingenuity of detail frequently indicates the severe contradictions of their mandate to bring conflicting
views "into harmony" *without deviating from
the route.*

In Leakin Park and Gwynns Falls valley, for
example, to "integrate the road into rolling
terrain and natural setting, minimize intru-
sion for park-users, and create a roadway
experience in park for the driver," the team
recommended the use of weathering steel
for bridges "to give a natural weathered appearance". If their recommendations are followed, the great lawn of the Crimea estate of
Victorian railroad engineer and entrepreneur
Thomas Winans will be reconstructed after cut-
and-cover construction of a 600 foot tunnel.
Special irrigation will be installed and the grade
in the tunnel will match the terrain so that
"the driver is exposed to the shape of the
park above". Barrier lighting will minimize
"spill light" in the park. A new channel for
Gwynn's Run will "simulate" the present
natural channel in every respect.

Entrances to the city will be landscaped and lighting will "create areas of night-time interest" and "edge" residential and industrial areas. High pole lighting will be used where spill light is not considered a problem and "peach color" sodium vapor lights will delineate and differentiate certain types of intersections. Plans were recommended for stockpiling topsoil. The swampy landscape of Moore's Run (on the east side) will be improved by planting "weeping specimens."

The Concept Team recognized explicitly the problem of scale. The road is a new large scale phenomenon, like the newest downtown buildings (USF&G, World Trade Center, or state office complex), the newest port installations, and town developments like Columbia and Cold Spring. All these phenomena reflect the transformation of the entire urban fabric into a new metro-scale structure. This scale may be called heroic or inhuman to suit one's bias, but in either case it does not match the existing neighborhoods, buildings, and service systems. The problem exists in all cities developed over several generations. In both downtown renewal and expressways, Baltimoreans of the 1960s and 1970s—business leader, professional, and the man in the street—have in different ways expressed the values of the human-scale city and resisted the inhuman more effectively than the "high brow" cities of Boston, Chicago, and San Francisco.

The problem of integrating the road into the "complex human scale of the neighborhood" is most acute in the Fell's Point-Canton corridor, the Franklin-Mulberry corridor, and the inner boulevard. In Fell's Point, a high structure of concrete precast box girder or voided concrete was proposed, with a "bright underside" because it will have foot traffic and a playground underneath the expressway. Twenty-five to thirty historic structures of the 1790s will be moved "to a better neighborhood." "How do you move a row house?" one stubborn citizen kept asking. Acoustical barriers are "for the first time being systematically applied" where a residential area would suffer an increase greater than six dBA. In Fell's Point they are to be transparent, although at other locations "acoustical fence" includes six foot sheet metal siding.

In the Franklin-Mulberry corridor a depressed roadway was recommended, with platform buildings—school, health center, and pedestrian overpasses—"to restore severed movement patterns." Its inbound traffic will pour onto a distributor bypass or boulevard, "something less than a freeway, but more than a street." It is designed for 30,000 vehicles per day, fifty mph design speed, and thirty mph average speed. The Concept Team recommended a system of parking corridors and large parking structures along the boulevard and at its junction with Franklin-Mulberry. The boulevard is also described as "a development tool," and its route is studded with joint development projects—the gems of federal subsidy held out to compensate impacted neighborhoods. Among the impacted areas are over 2,000 units of public housing. Here, at the junction of corridor and boulevard, many of the persons displaced from the corridor have been relocated. This appears to be the most alarming zone for air pollution.

SYSTEM THINKING

The theory of the Concept Team was system and careful attention was paid to consistent systemwide signs, safety design, and traffic monitoring, as well as lighting, planting, and aesthetic detail. It now appears, however, that the chief defects of the 3-A modified system and of the Concept Team's work lie in weaknesses of system thinking.

First, in the area of environmental impact, air pollution and noise problems were grossly understated because of segmented consideration. The federal Environmental Protection Agency protested in 1973 that they considered the environmental impact statements wholly inadequate because there was not enough attention to the overall system. Baltimore was supposed to reduce its carbon monoxide pollution level by 50 percent by 1975, but the expressway plans project an increase of automobiles coming into the central district. The concentration of pollution in the central district will be intensified, and it is necessary to consider *jointly* the effects of the several problem segments which compose an inner-loop—the Franklin-Mulberry, the boulevard, and the segment of I-83 which runs down the Fallsway toward Fell's Point. There are also difficult problems of air pollution involved in the Fort McHenry crossing, associated with the combination of industrial pollution and bridge approach. Expensive design detail could not compensate for the failure to consider environmental impact in the original location of the highways.

Air pollution and noise problems are associated with the operation of the system at its most intense levels. Yet official public reports are still reluctant to discuss the peak hour parameters. There have been well-argued accusations that the "delicately balanced" system may break down altogether under rush hour operations. The crucial points appear to be the major central interchanges and the boulevards by which traffic is to be dispersed into the old downtown street network. Innumerable schemes have been proposed for inner harbor crossings. One called for "two mammoth spaghetti-filled interchanges" less than a mile apart. Another required a fourteen lane bridge shaped like a cube. Still another proposed an expressway tunnel which would have collided with a planned mass transit tunnel. An inner habor crossing was finally abandoned and the Fort McHenry crossing adopted.

Doubts also remain as to whether the total system is needed. Superhighway planning is largely self-justifying—the traffic will go wherever you build the road. Because all hearings were rigidly focused upon a particular segment, just as the environmental impact statements were, the overall traffic handling of the system could not be fully debated. Assumptions shifted continuously as to whether a particular segment would serve through traffic or Baltimore traffic. No segment was designed to serve local or neighborhood traffic and it is clear that the basic problem is one of redistribution: the benefits and costs are not spread over the same people. The redistribution problem is therefore the fundamental geopolitical issue, and the effort to manipulate, soften, or conceal the costs has led to mistrust and fiscal distortion. City and state juggled traffic, street repair, and policing funds in order to conceal road costs. The state issued $23 million in bonds for the city's 12 percent share, because state bonds do not require voter approval, whereas city bonds do. City voters repeatedly rejected bonds for a relocation of police headquarters to express their opposition to the road, but the city administration built it anyway.

In November 1971 several councilmen were elected as expressway opponents and when they took office (January) a public hearing was staged in a small room of the public library. By this time, as the housing commissioner expressed it, "We [had] suffered most of the negative effects of the expressway and none of the benefits." The city had spent $50 million on the Jones Falls Expressway, $100 million on the 3-A system, had relocated at least 4,000 households, and demolished or depreciated three major corridors. The new system price tag exceeded $1 billion. At the hearing it was clear that "system" was a political idea—selling the package. The technical personnel, the municipal administration, and the Greater Baltimore Committee lobbyist argued that the system was so well integrated that removing any part would destroy its functioning—i.e., take it or leave it. The MAD coalition opposed the system: "We don't want NO road." This position was inevitable, in view of their experience of divide-and-conquer tactics, the politics of coalition, and the profound mistrust of the "highwaymen." The chairman of the city Planning Commission was not allowed to speak at the twelve hour hearing and the next day he resigned, regretting among other features this polarization:

> Nowhere was there to be found the rational middle ground—the case for *some* expressways. This case is solid. The one for a complete system is not. . . . The hearings were, in effect, one more charade in the history of the expressway saga. (*Baltimore Sun,* February 19, 1972)

Construction continues as a large pincers movement, boring in relentlessly on the controversial segments.

AUTOMOBILE-ORIENTED SETTLEMENT

Meanwhile, in spite of "systemwide" planning, a somewhat different system has gradually emerged. We have seen how massive relocation generated strong resistance (negative feedback), delaying numerous sections of the expressway program and diverting location. More important were positive feedbacks associated with the larger growth of the city, creating patterns of automobile-oriented settlement. The changes in settlement and mobility which occurred in the Baltimore region in the 1960s and which appear likely in the 1970s are classic examples of

Myrdal's circular cumulative causation. There are now 700,000 cars in the region. Virtually the entire labor force in the suburban counties drives to work. Only in the city do a substantial number of people go to work by bus. Only two-thirds of city residents now work in the city. The populations of Anne Arundel and Howard counties increased faster than the number of jobs there and they generate substantial flows toward the Washington metropolitan area as well as to Baltimore.

The automobile made possible the settlement of the suburban counties and the settlement of the suburban counties generates the demand for shorter travel time, more parking spaces, and more road for peak hour commuting. Figures 26 and 27 give some idea of the magnitude of the reciprocal movement—resi-

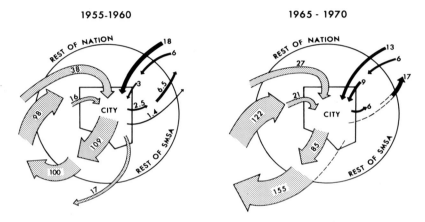

Figure 26. Migration streams by race, in thousands of moves during the five year interval. Residential movement between the suburban counties and the rest of the nation have intensified, but there was little change in the pattern. Blacks are underrepresented in all moves between counties, especially moves into the suburban ring. Moves out of the region are not reported in detail for 1970, but the majority of white outmigrants are from the counties, while the majority of black outmigrants are from the city. Source: U.S. Census.

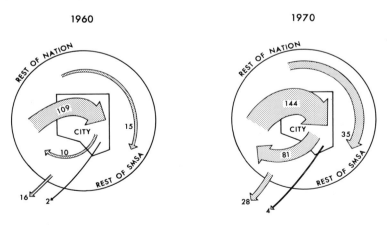

Figure 27. The journey to work, 1960 and 1970. Changes in the pattern of daily journeys to work result from the combined effects of residential moves (Figure 26) and the creation of new jobs. Commuting into the city has increased despite small growth of jobs in the city. Commuting from the city to the suburban counties and between adjoining suburban counties has increased markedly. Source: U.S. Census.

dential moves to the suburbs and daily commuter trips to the center. The kind of feedback involved here was pinpointed in a Regional Planning Council study of the situation at Social Security in 1970. Two-thirds drove their own cars, half alone; 28 percent were car pool passengers, and only 6 percent rode buses. Back in 1966, only a quarter of the employees drove to work alone. The changes resulted from the federal government having developed free and unrestricted employee parking, about 8,000 spaces, at $4,500 per space. Downtown likewise the city's off street parking commission has subsidized 8,000 garage spaces (since 1948) through low interest municipal revenue bonds and a property tax subsidy for the duration of the loans.

In spite of gasoline prices, there is every reason to believe that the process will continue. The Regional Planning Council forecasts rapid residential settlement of the outlying areas over the next ten to fifteen years in Howard and Harford counties and accelerated growth of jobs in Anne Arundel and Howard counties. This may limit the movements in and out of the city, but it will favor more beltway traffic and other movements within and between the suburban counties. Road development in the counties reinforces our expectation. Expressway type development extends much beyond the interstate highway system. A crisscross of limited access roads is consuming much land and fragmenting still larger areas, particularly in the coastal plain corridor of Baltimore County and Anne Arundel County.

Meanwhile, the problem will become yet more acute for the city dwellers without cars. The whole inner city becomes a low level trap —you cannot move out without a car and a steady job. You cannot get a job without a car. Yet the inner residential core without cars is the zone which has borne the impact of relocation and will now bear the greatest air pollution, noise, interruption to foot traffic—in short the greatest inconvenience from the secondary effects of other people's mobility (Figure 28).

WHAT ABOUT MASS TRANSIT?

The critical decision seems to have been made that Baltimore will have a mass transit high speed rail system. The price tag discussed in 1973 was $1.5 billion and rising. A first leg will

connect downtown Baltimore with Reisterstown to the northwest and Glen Burnie and Friendship Airport to the south. But so far the public has not shown much interest (relocation is small) and does not believe that the system will materialize. Even the gasoline crisis of 1973 did not build up a head of steam.

The mass transit system is not designed as a substitute, but as a supplement to a highway sytem. Suburban commuters are expected to continue to own automobiles and are likely to use them to commute to the mass transit stations. The projected network of feeder buses is designed only for service intervals of thirty minutes in "high density" residential areas and an hour in other parts of the region. One segment will run in a median of the Northwest Expressway, apparently to help justify the construction of the highway (state-funded). Traffic expectations for 1990 (as of 1962) were that the expressway will be overloaded, with a capacity of 45,000 cars a day, while the transit line will be underutilized, with 13,000 passengers a day, a capacity of 60,000 per hour.

The overall system is conceived as a planning tool which will concentrate high-rise and commercial development around the stations, reinforcing the concepts of a Metro Center (downtown Baltimore), town centers and sector centers in the counties, and a corridor development pattern in higher density population ridges. It is expected to reinforce certain high value nodal locations and speculative opportunities (near the beltway and the inner boulevard).

In spite of the advantages, it is difficult to juggle the transit plans to make them equally attractive to both the city and the counties, anxious about cost sharing. An Anne Arundel county councilman said (1971), "A rapid-rail transit system designed primarily to serve downtown Baltimore must rank very low on our list of priorities." Yet to obtain support of city interests, convenience for downtown commuters and shoppers is billed as essential to downtown revitalization. All lines will radiate from a central station under Charles Center.

The overall mass transit strategy resembles the highway strategy. Its first objective is to capture the federal dollar. Two-thirds of the cost was expected to be paid by federal funds and intense pressures were built up "to maintain the rhythm of planning." In 1974 new interest in commuter adaptations of the rail-

Figure 28. The sump and the alabaster city. The Inner Harbor is the sink for untreated surface drainage from highways, and residues of oil, gasoline, zinc, and lead. More oil goes into the harbor from accidents and negligence on land than from vessels. This sump of water pollution is an old vexation. A century ago, before sanitary sewers were built, the issue was the summer stink. It is small, artificially deepened, and has a "three-layered" tidal circulation. Beck estimates that now the coliform bacteria level (indicating sewage) is attributable to the feces of the city's 100,000 dogs. The Inner Harbor renewal program has provided momentum for research and for a serious effort at enforcing water pollution laws.

roads was suddenly sparked by hopes of federal subsidy. *Both* road and rail transport programs have suffered from distorted priorities because of three-layered financing, three-layered technocracy, and county-city rivalries. They also suffer from more fundamental problems. We have seen how closely the settlement pattern and the transportation pattern are related. But housing is handled as a private sector for production and consumption, while transportation is treated as a massively subsidized or public sector. The essential question is, How are the costs and benefits from public subsidy distributed? The intensity of the expressway controversy suggests that either we do not all have the same expectations or else we do not all agree the redistribution is just

City on the Falls

Baltimore's "fall line" location is the key to understanding its environmental assets—for industrial, residential, and recreational development. It is also the key to its environmental problems and politics. Baltimore is typical of the East Coast metropolitan areas strung along the fall line geological contact between the old uplands and the Atlantic coastal plain.

The physiographic term *fall line* refers to the fall of the streams, here usually fifty to one hundred feet over a stretch ten or fifteen miles, which allowed the development of water powered mills for grinding wheat into flour, later converted for making cotton duck sailcloth. The several "runs" or "falls"—the Patapsco, the Gwynn's Falls, Jones' Falls, Herring Run, and the Great and the Little Gunpowder falls—cross the geologic zone of contact, roughly from northwest to southeast, to flow into the Chesapeake Bay. As elsewhere, the millstreams were gradually abandoned as a major source of industrial energy. They became sewers for carrying off slaughterhouse wastes or were dammed for water supply reservoirs. As sources of energy, they were replaced by massive new industrial fuels introduced from outside the region and from the underground "stores": Appalachian coal and oil, then Venezuelan oil, natural gas, and nuclear power. The boost in total energy applied is a major factor in environmental crises. The dissipation of most of this energy is still handled by the basic gravity flow systems—underground and surface drainage, the circulation of warm and

cool water in the bay, and warm and cool air in the atmosphere. Each of the two natural landscapes—piedmont and coastal plain—provides distinctive raw materials for human use and each forms a distinctive warp and woof into which man weaves his routes and pipes and wires. Just as the old row house grids still form a matrix for social sorting and social movement, the basic physiographic structure is still the matrix for the sorting and movement of material and energy.

The beautiful rolling piedmont provided a variety of building stones—marble for the steps, granite for the basilica, greenstone for Mount Vernon Place Methodist Church, sandstone for Franklin Street Presbyterian. It offered a wealth of local plant environments—white oak on the plateaus of Wissahickon schist, post oak and scrub pine barrens on the serpentine, pure stands of beech in the coves, sycamores on the valley floors. Each knoll or hilltop grove was first appreciated as a gentleman's estate or summer place and in later generations turned into subdivision, park or cemetery—Beech Hill, Chestnut Ridge, Marble Hill, Druid Hill, Green Mount. The valleys of that piedmont landscape have for seventy-five years been seen as a regional system of linear parks and parkways. The Olmsted brothers' plan of 1903, commissioned by the Municipal Art Society, was wonderfully sensitive to the rocks, trees, and landscapes unique to each piedmont valley. Thanks to reservoir development and the Civilian Conservation Corps in the 1930s, park development was most fully carried out in the Patapsco and Gunpowder Falls valleys. Each now has 10,000 acres in park and twenty miles of nature trails.

The old mill roads such as Falls Road and Franklintown Road and parkways of the 1920s such as Ellicott Driveway, Wyman Park Drive, and Chinquapin Parkway harmonized with the stream valley park concept, but expressways have been harder to blend in. The earliest successful linear park, along Gwynn's Falls, will be dismembered by an expressway. In the Jones Falls valley an expressway was completed, but the imaginative park plan (by David Wallace) miscarried. The Jones Falls mill dams, wild strawberries, and butterflies remain secret places of people who explore railroad yards.

The coastal plain, trending northeast-southwest, is Baltimore's great transport corridor to the rest of Megalopolis and the bay is its corridor to the rest of the world. The region's industries use the quaternary sediments of the coastal plain as ground water reservoirs and mine the sands and gravels for concrete, the clays for making brick and fire-brick. In former times they also recovered iron nodules. Where the streams enter the unconsolidated coastal plain materials they become broad and sluggish and are called rivers or creeks instead of runs or falls. Herring Run, for example, becomes the Back River. The rivers and margins of the Chesapeake contain the wetlands or tidal marshes important to the life cycles of blue crab, oyster, clam, menhaden, striped bass, and shad and to the weekend and seasonal recreation flux of the human population.

THE VULNERABLE FRINGE

Knowing that much biological and chemical exchange takes place in the interfaces—the earth's "thin skin" of soil between air and rock, and the coastal margins between continent and ocean—we can expect to find in the Baltimore region a critical biological zone along the tidal margins of the rivers and the bay—its piers and channels, its mudflats and wetlands. There is amazing variation from place to place, from hour to hour, and from season to season in temperature, salinity, and sediment content. The bay is vast and shallow, "paper thin" if we reduce it to a small model. Its variations provide a richness of niches for water life. This wealth of the necks and rivers landscape was as easily recognized by explorers and settlers as

the potential value of the falls. Muskrat trapping, duck hunting, and crabbing, already familiar to the Nanticoke, the Suquehannock, and the Piscataway Indians, promptly became the basis for economic and recreational values of both rich and poor.

But each local environment, each species' life cycle, each food chain is vulnerable to sudden change. Immense investments have taken place in the coastal plain. Industrial development implies concentrated application of energy and harbor development implies massive changes in the dimensions of the bay—filling whole coves and dredging to new depths. Each lump of capital has had important impacts on the ecosystem and has fired political controversy, scientific research, and popular environmental concern.

Channel and port development programs posed an urgent problem of disposal of spoil—dredged harbor mud (Figure 29). The dredging of the fifty foot channel and the container facilities was stymied for over two years because a site could not be agreed upon for dumping 2.3 million cubic yards of mud. (Another two million yards will be dredged annually as maintenance.) Older sites—deep places in the bay at Kent Island and Poole's Island—had been filled. The material is fine silt with 60 percent water. It is not easily compacted and drained and is not usable as fill for construction sites. Because the upper layer, perhaps a third, is contaminated by oil, lead, cadmium, molybdenum, nickel, manganese, and cobalt (but little mercury, in contrast to dredge fill elsewhere), the U.S. Environmental Protection Agency was opposed to dumping it in the bay without dikes to contain it. Over vigorous protest, the port authority finally chose the Hart and Miller Island area for a diked spoil disposal which will cost $13 million and take three or four years to build.

Except for the contaminants, the dredging spoils resemble deposits from the natural processes of hydrology, erosion, and sedimentation in the bay. The Susquehanna River, mighty tributary at the head of the bay, normally brings down one-half to one million cubic yards of sediment a year, but runoff and sediment occasionally increase dramatically. For example, in June 1972, the Susquehanna, swollen from hurricane Agnes, created new mud flats and chains of islands. The bay is the "drowned valley of the ancestral Susquehanna," and its

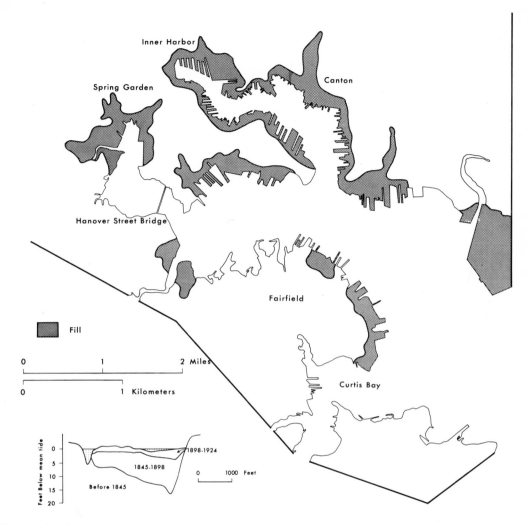

Figure 29. Sedimentation in Baltimore Harbor. Original shore line and sedimentation since time of colonial settlement were mapped by the Maryland Geological Survey. The cross section at Hanover Street bridge is from L. C. Gottschalk, *Geographical Review*, 1945.

complex ecosystem depends on gradual tidal mixing to produce the full range of salinity, from fresh water to sea water. The unusual outflow of fresh water caused by Hurricane Agnes killed oysters and clams (they require about five parts salt per thousand) and apparently contributed to fish kills from oxygen depletion in the brackish layer underneath. The Conowingo power dam on the Susquehanna is regulated with attention to that problem of oxygen distribution. There is concern that flows in the bay may be seriously affected by

deepening of the C & D Canal and diversion to Baltimore of more water from the Susquehanna River.

Nearly $1 billion was invested in power plants for the Baltimore area in the early 1970s and the environment effects are concentrated in the tidewater fringe. Baltimore Gas and Electric Company has developed a nuclear plant at Calvert Cliffs, in Calvert County to the south. Another is planned for near the mouth of the C & D Canal to the north. PEPCO (Potomac Edison) will build two others on the bay to serve the Washington metropolitan area. The constuction costs included millions "to protect the environment." Risks of accident and problems of disposal of plutonium wastes remain controversial issues, as elsewhere in the nation. But the everyday impact on the bay is merely an aggravation of that of other power plants. Because the efficiency of nuclear plants is less than that of fossil-fueled plants, more waste heat is disposed of to the water. A liquefied natural gas plant was built in the city and a gas turbine power plant at Perryman (Harford County). A large plant was built at the mouth of the Conemaugh coal mine in western Maryland, but the several older coal-burning plants around the Inner Harbor and Spring Garden were converted to oil because in the late sixties oil was the cheaper fuel and cheaper in terms of emission control. Ironically, some of the coal-handling equipment was actually scrapped just in time for the oil shortage and price increases precipitated by the Arab oil embargo of 1973.

Bethlehem Steel at Sparrows Point offers, as we might expect from it size, an example of the many effects of industrial energy use on the environment. It uses ten million tons of iron ore in a year, five million tons of coal, and much larger tonnages of water and air. It uses seven million gallons a day of filtered city water, larger amounts of well water, and circulates 700 million gallons of brackish harbor water for cooling and quenching. It releases great quantities of heat to the atmosphere as well as to the bay. But Bethlehem is also an example of the pressures and efforts involved in controlling such emissions and recycling materials. Bethlehem is part of a complex urban ecosystem. New electrostatic precipitators collect 167 tons of usable iron oxide dust daily from the open hearth furnaces. The city delivers 300 to 400 abandoned cars a day to a monster car shredder which in turn supplies scrap to Bethlehem. The steel company generates electricity from surplus blast furnace gas, coke breeze, and fuel oil and participates in the regional electric power pool with BG&E. Bethlehem delivers its slag to a specially built plant of the Arundel Corporation for making road materials. Most remarkable is Bethlehem's purchase of the entire treated effluent of the city's principal sewage treatment plant—130 million gallons a day. The use of the effluent as an industrial water supply was devised to overcome ground water problems which be-

came severe during the industrial spurt of World War II, as the entire industrial area can be considered one great well. Intensive pumping caused the water table to drop radically, brackish water began to move into ground water aquifers, and Bethlehem was forced to seek an alternative source of fresh water.

Current problems at the giant steel plant relate to deterioration of surface water quality. In 1970 the state stepped up its pressure on Bethlehem to control effluents contributing to fish kills. Among the illegal discharges were cyanide, phenols and oils from the coke oven and benzol plants, and zinc and cadmium from the wire mill. Bethlehem attributes a tenth of its recent investment program to pollution abatement. The Baltimore County Council has arranged for the company to use the county's federal tax-exempt status to issue $28 million in low interest bonds to finance air and water pollution control devices.

CLEANING UP THE BACK YARD

In Baltimore's more affluent nineteenth century neighborhoods, the front and back of a row house symbolized a lifestyle. The fronts had bay windows, marble stoops, wide streets with sidewalks and street trees. In back, lining the ten foot alley, were the privies and stables, old "summer kitchens," dwellings of servants and laborers, the board fences, garbage cans and flies, and the gutters draining from kitchen and laundry. Many of the horrors of alley environments have been eliminated, notably typhus and infant cholera. Some of the factors of improvement have been the disappearance of the urban horse, the change from soft coal to fuel oil, underground sewering, and machinery built into houses—the toilet, washing machine, drier, and garbage disposal unit. The alleys were paved with cement and gradually the dwellings were removed from them. Postwar neighborhoods of garden apartments have layouts such that one can hardly tell which is the front or back of the row.

But modernized evacuation of wastes from neighborhoods requires sites for processing and disposal—sewage treatment for 200 million gallons a day, dumping grounds for 2,500 tons of solid waste a day, reprocessing for waste oil, a rendering plant for disposal of 30,000 dead dogs and cats a year. These activities were concentrated in certain tidal margins which we might call Baltimore's back yards or the alleys of twentieth century affluence. In East Baltimore, along Back River, are the region's largest sewage treatment plant and its largest incinerator. Off Back River are the old sludge disposal sites and the new sites for diked spoil. In the southwest, where Gwynn's Falls flows into Spring Garden, once the site of a white lead works, we find bus junk yards, the Westport powerplant, and the new liquefied natural gas plant. In the south, on the Patapsco River mud flats, are the often offensive Reedbird incinerator and landfill.

Baltimore has accelerated its efforts in the 1970s to reclaim and relandscape its back yards. What has been accomplished? The sewage treatment plant at Back River is being rebuilt to increase its capacity and the flexibility of its processes. It is one of the largest trickling filter plants in the world. These photogenic rotating sprinklers are displayed in a wooded park open to the public (drive out Eastern Avenue). Low-sudsing detergents have eliminated the great suds which for years blew or flowed over Back River. Nearby, an ancient private dump "of last resort," long a site for the sport of nighttime rat shooting, was plowed up in 1973. A stratum of cockroaches was treated with chemicals. The terrain was totally reconstructed and aggregate was added to support a landscaped expressway interchange.

In the lower Gwynn's Falls valley, the city has just built a spectacular new pyrolysis plant —an incinerator of high temperatures, more complete combustion, elaborate sorting, and reclamation. Metals will feed Bethlehem; the glass will be used for road-paving material. (A sample of the glinting surface, glasphalt, can be seen on downtown Charles Street.) The process will produce enough methane to operate the plant and sell surplus steam to the BG&E steam plant, which supplies heat to downtown buildings. The pyrolysis plant, the first of its type and scale in the nation, was sited to eliminate auto junkyards and private dumps at the city's Washington Parkway entrance. The pyrolysis plant will also allow the city to phase out the Reedbird incinerator in South Baltimore. The adjoining Patapsco mudflats are gradually being developed as parkland.

THE CORE ENVIRONMENT

The city's original site astride the geologic contact zone and astride the millstreams makes it the hub of the transport system of the state, and places it in a critical position in the gravity flow systems of drainage, sanitation, and sedimentation. As in other fall line cities, its old and central location—that is, the "core" properties of Baltimore—adds to its specific environmental problems and aggravates and conflicts with less built-up and more peripheral parts of the region. The very nature of a city is to concentrate people, goods, and information, to facilitate their exchange. At the core of the region, and in the core of the city itself, land values tend to be high, intensities of movement are great, and buildings are tall. Because this core has developed over a long period of time, some elements of its structure are obsolete or deteriorated and there are complex vested interests.

The core is, for example, the center of the metropolitan "heat dome," a basic urban modification of the circulation of air and air pollutants. This is a factor increasing heat stress for people close to the core during extreme meteorological conditions—the summertime heat wave. Columbia, the "new town" in Howard County, appears to be a small scale developmental model of the full blown urban heat dome and air pollution system of Baltimore itself. In 1967 only 200 people lived on the 28 square kilometers of the town. By 1970 there were 10,000, by 1974 35,000. (The population target is 100,000.) Helmut Landsberg has documented the development and expansion of the urban heat island, with nighttime summer temperature differentials of 4.5°C between "downtown" Columbia and the countryside, a 4 percent decrease in relative humidity (daytime), a decrease of vapor pressure, and a greater recirculation of city air. He attributes the changes primarily to the replacement of vegetation with paved and shingled surfaces and the resulting changes in the rates at which heat flows into and out of the soil. Buildings also block wind and renewal of air. Baltimore City, by virtue of its greater size, taller buildings at the center, and much more complete coverage with asphalt paving and roofs, has stronger differentials. The metropolitan area is so varied in configuration and land use that the climatologist John Lewis (of McGill University, formerly of the University of Maryland) has been able to relate the profile of heat radiation to land use features. On infrared photographs Bethlehem Steel stands out as a distinct "heat island," while Druid Hill Park appears as an "oasis."

The major distinctions of form which we observed in Baltimore's social geography—coastal plain and piedmont, green wedge and suburban circle—appear to match patterns of variation in the basic environmental resources, and in particular the distribution of extreme environmental stresses. In Baltimore, mortality has always been highest in the hot months of July and August, although the recognized "causes of death" have changed from generation to generation. In spite of anxiety over "hot summers," there is still limited public information about the significance of urban microclimates to murder and mass violence. The murder rate radically increased in Baltimore in 1972 and has stayed up. Homicide accounts for 3 percent of deaths in the city. We do know that these phenomena are concentrated in the inner city asphalt core, as are air pollution, lead, rats, noise, and lung diseases. There phenomena have provoked highly emotional responses and curiously erratic control efforts. For example, year after year the city health department issued congratulatory reports on the steady decline of lead poisoning cases among children—down to seven or eight in 1973. But a strong research program of national importance had just begun in Baltimore in 1972 and the new evidence reveals thousands of cases of lead poisoning. Thirty percent of inner city children (both black and white) have higher blood levels of lead than is considered safe.

Another example of uncertain and emotional priorities is animal control. Baltimore, with federal assistance and in response to the intense emotional response of inner city residents, spent several millions on rat control and related sanitation problems in the 1970s. But there are fifty or sixty rat bites in the city each year and 7,000 dog bites. Dog bites have increased 50 percent since 1960. Baltimore was the research area for Alan Beck's ecological study of the urban "free-ranging" dog. He estimates the population of strays at 40,000 and pet dogs at perhaps 60,000. They present serious health threats, notably the transmission of tuberculosis and a worm which can cause blindness. The number of large dogs and potential biters (according to breed, sex, and degree of confinement) has increased in response to anxiety about crime. "Nearly every back yard bordering the alleys of Baltimore contains a captive dog," Beck reports. Stray dogs live in vacant houses, turn over garbage cans, and chase the cats who kill the rats. Dog feces are food for rats, breeding places of flies, and carriers of parasitic diseases. Dogs and children compete for space.

Children and elderly persons are most vulnerable to carbon monoxide, sulphur dioxide, heat stress, noise (interrupted sleep), and infections. They are also the prime pedestrian targets for automobiles. Pedestrian environments have deteriorated generally, in spite of unusual research effort by the city planning department on the social uses of the streets, and special planning in renewal areas. More garage and service entrances interrupt sidewalks than before. Automobile exhaust and traffic noise are most intense at pedestrian levels. Grades and approaches are controlled more rigorously for motor vehicles than for pedestrians and users of wheelchairs. Many suburban areas do not require sidewalks. Their shopping centers have protected pedestrian malls inside the treacherous zone of unpoliced vehicle traffic.

One response to the various environmental hazards has been the escape into sealed-off environments with air conditioning and wholly artificial lighting. However, the effects of such environments on behavior, health, and mental health are uncertain. Public schools and infant day care centers have been built without windows. Apartment houses, residences for the elderly, and nursing homes all feature maximum uniformity or control in the environment and total cutoff from weather, natural stimuli, and people outside.

All of those neglected or newly discovered environmental deficiencies affect above all the people who live in the core. The inner city concentration of the poor, the elderly, the black, public housing tenants, and children dependent on public assistance for food and medical care is associated with the strong concentration of heat, noise, lead, dog feces, broken glass, carbon monoxide, sulfur dioxide, and exceptional deficiencies of grass, shade, and privacy. Just as in the nineteenth century alleys, the tendency remains for certain populations—physically vulnerable, economically marginal, politically weak—to bear the hard to measure or hard to predict environmental costs.

PROBLEMS ARISING IN
THE PERIPHERY

Environmental problems also occur in the periphery where there have been radical jumps in population, energy inputs, mobility, and intensity of land use. This is true of the residential, industrial, and recreational land uses in the periphery. The problems are associated with investment leads and lags. The total growth of the region produces system overloads, most apparent in "downstream" environments.

Most of the recent residential growth has occurred on the piedmont, upstream from the city which was founded on the harbor. Regional sanitary sewers generally run downhill to the big treatment plant at Back River and the new Patapsco plant. Likewise, the storm drainage of Baltimore and Anne Arundel counties courses through the city. This means that any defects in the disposal of these effluents has repercussions in the city. From time to time the state health department has declared moratoria on issuing building permits in parts of Baltimore County, in order to limit the severe overloading of sanitary sewers and "overflow" sewage pollution of the Gwynn's Falls and the Jones Falls in the city.

Half the dwellings of Anne Arundel, Howard, and Harford counties depend on septic tanks for sewage disposal (see Figure 23). They are the same areas which rely on ground water for domestic supply.

> We are spending millions of dollars in the eastern part of the county providing water and sewers. At the same time, we are letting subdivisions go into the rural areas where they are beyond the reasonable water and sewers and certainly sometime in the future a problem is going to develop there because the septic tank sooner or later will fail. With good maintenance and good soil conditions it can last for many years without troubles, but sooner or later the soil becomes fully saturated.
>
> (U.S. Civil Rights Commission Hearing)

Suburban development has produced sizable changes in storm drainage parameters. Storm drainage is handled mainly by the "natural" stream channels. The same manmade radiating surfaces which create a change of heat flux and circulation of the air also produce changes in the flux of water into the ground and in the surface runoff. The runoff from urbanized watersheds with mostly paved or roofed surfaces is much swifter than from wooded or grassed surfaces or even from plowed land. Therefore, in the Maryland pattern of heavy summer rain-

storms, the runoff peaks are swifter and more intense, producing more frequent flash floods and aggravating the rare events such as Hurricane Agnes (June 1972) when twelve inches of rain fell in one day. The flood damage also occurred downstream.

The hazards of work environments have not yet become a major public issue in Baltimore, although the metropolitan area presumably has a cross-section of the problems of other regions, such as excessive noise levels, unlabeled chemicals, acid spills, and noxious dusts and fumes. Many of those subjected to maximum hazards are workers in the outer harbor—construction workers and those in heavy metal manufacturing, oil and chemical plants, and paints. Blue collar census tracts in the city and in eastern Baltimore County have the highest rates in the region for disability among persons of working age. Many disabilities and chronic illnesses are never traced to their work environment sources.

The first indication of work environment hazards more severe in the Baltimore region than elsewhere comes from recent epidemiological studies of cancer. Mason and McKay's statistics of cancer deaths by counties of the U.S., 1950 to 1969, reveal decided excesses for Baltimore City in certain cancers which have elsewhere been linked to handling of specific industrial chemicals (carcinogens such as vinyl chloride). Men's city rates for cancers of the bladder and kidney and the more common cancer of the lung run 50 percent higher than state and national averages. (These contrast with rather low local rates for cancers of stomach and brain, and women's averages for cancer of the breast and cervix.) Radford's more specific study of 1973–1974 deaths among employees and pensioners of the Bethlehem Steel Sparrows Point plant shows still higher death rates in precisely the same categories. The rates for the population of steelworkers over age thirty-five ran 50 percent higher than what would be expected from city averages, already 50 percent higher than national averages.

Those initial results are especially interesting because they also indicate the life and death significance of the social structure of the job market and the social space in the factory. The distinctive distribution of jobs by race at the steel plant discussed earlier was matched by sharply different incidence of cancer deaths —kidney and liver cancers among blacks, bladder cancers among whites. "Excess deaths" were greater among whites, more of whom had served at least twenty years in a particular sector of the plant. Among the shipyard workers there were more deaths from lung cancer (and other respiratory diseases), consistent with their known exposure to asbestos. The new trend toward hiring blacks and women in a wider range of jobs ironically exposes them to new hazards. New industrial techniques have also introduced new risks—such as exposure to powered chromium salts in chrome plating— whose consequences have not yet shown up in death statistics. Once again, Bethlehem is merely an example, better documented because of its size and union concern, but indicative of conditions in other firms. Baltimore's very old copper and chrome smelting plants which shut down in the early seventies have left contaminated areas on the north rim of the harbor (Fell's Point, Canton, Highlandtown). On the south rim (Fairfield and Curtis Bay), dusts and fumes are frequent signs hinting at the invisible hazards within the plants. Hazards increased in the boom of the late sixties and early seventies when oil and chemical industries were working to capacity and overloading their systems. 1973-1975 layoffs undermined the bargaining position of employees.

We have seen how residential construction and industrial growth generate environmental changes on the periphery that have powerful impacts downstream and at the urban core— floods, deaths, disability payments, medicare costs. Likewise, if we look at the recreational zone still farther out on the periphery, we shall see a chain of impact which reaches again all the way to the core. What appear to be distinguishing traits of the periphery and the core are two sides of the same coin. Environmental problems on the periphery and environmental deficiencies in the core boil down to the same basic problem of access. Maryland's extraordinary variety of scenery, wildlife, and water life had survived in its piedmont stream valleys and tidewater wetlands because of their remoteness or high costs of draining and building. Less wetland, for example, has been lost than in other states, even though nearly all of it is privately owned. But carownership, roadbuilding, and a shorter work week have suddenly made these distant resources beyond the metropolitan region more accessible to more people and converted the elite styles of recreation such as duck hunting and sailing into mass activities. The new accessibility has posed new problems. The intensity of recreation

activities reduces some of the recreational values. Hunting has become so popular that the sport is risky for the hunters. Fishing has become a collective rather than a solitary pastime at Loch Raven, Broening Park, and Curtis Bay. Holidays and summer weekends are traffic jams at the Bay Bridge and campgrounds have become quasiurban installations. Recent projects for Worcester County wetlands include a "campominium" on a thousand acres, with six campsites per acre, a trailer park for a thousand trailers, and a resort camp of 3,300 acres. Machine access to recreation sites threatens even the survival of recreation environments. The newly acquired National Seashore on Assateague Island must rigidly restrict camper vehicles, cars, and dune buggies because of the danger of having its fragile dunes erode. Coastal erosion would follow. At Ocean City, land costs have shot up, private hold on the entire beach is reinforced, and high-rise construction now aims at luxury condominiums and year round convention business, while family vacation use is diminished.

But the more distant recreation opportunities have not been equally accessible to everyone. New problems of distribution have emerged, revealing the connection between development problems at the core and the periphery. Because the new mobility is *auto* mobility, the recreation gap has widened between people with and without cars. Streetcar lines and electrics no longer offer access to commercial swimming pools and amusement parks. Growth of harbor and industrial activity has fenced off or polluted more of the causal crabbing, boating, bathing, and fishing places. Community associations in the city's green wedge and in the suburbs have sponsored membership pools, but there are only the four sizable outdoor municipal swimming pools of 1920. Fifty small "portable" pools purchased after the 1968 riot were designed for regimented use by children and were spotted on blacktop playgrounds, but as the "hot summer" threat receded they have been left in mothballs. None was installed in 1974.

WHOSE ENVIRONMENT?

The problems described arise from the growth of the total Baltimore region—in population, wealth, energy use, and mobility. As the region develops, some resources become more abundant or accessible, others become more scarce or more costly. What makes these problems controversial is their distributional aspect. Who will share in the new abundance? Who will bear the added costs? We have seen how threats to the magnificent environmental resources of the bay arise from the scramble for site values and access. Each household, each neighborhood or identity group, each corporation enters a competition for environmental resources. Each struggles to capture benefits and evade costs. Consequently, environmental conflict is channeled by the legal and political framework. Property lines set up jurisdictions between householders. Political boundaries set up jurisdictions between groups of taxpayers. Environmental issues arise whenever resources or costs must be shared across these boundaries.

For example, developer proposals for extension of sewers into the areas around Loch Raven reservoir, Soldier's Delight, and the Worthington Valley raised the question of environmental planning. The debate hinged on the issue of distribution. The beautiful limestone valleys called Green Spring, Worthington, and Caves, some 45,000 acres, are part of the horsey country of gentleman farming north of Baltimore. A community council of 5,000 families invited Ian McHarg and David Wallace to develop a plan in 1962. Their plan would protect the more fragile environments. The steep valley walls would remain forested. The floodplain and open valleys on Cockeysville marble would be reserved for agriculture, pasture, and low intensity institutional open space. Residential development would be allowed on the wooded plateaus, with high-rise towers on the promontories. The planners showed that total land values would be greater than with "uncontrolled growth." While the proposal helped delay random subdivision, and has so far prevented the sewer extension, there has not yet been agreement on a program of implementation or redistribution of rising land values. In spite of their appreciation of use values of the habitat, the resident owners are committed to the game of individual private risk and private manipulation of market values.

The problem is similar in the tidewater zone. Virtually the entire tidewater margin of Maryland is private property, parceled into thousands of jurisdictions. In the city it is all zoned for industrial use; in Anne Arundel County most is zoned for low density residential use, accessed by private roads. Vacant sites remain with potential for recreation and other uses,

but all are "encumbered." In order to protect wetlands, state legislation was passed in 1970 establishing strong state powers and a permit system for all dredge and fill and some state enforcement has begun. One developer was obliged to restore a wetland site. This controversy was characteristic of the race between owners to capture new market values and other citizens to assert rights to user values.

How and where to provide water mains and sewers are issues which involve redistribution across county lines as well as among households. The developed city has excellent, well-integrated water and sewage treatment plants adequate for the next generation. These plants serve to some extent the suburban populations, which share in operating costs. But the fast-growing peripheral counties need to build systems of comparable size over the next twenty years. They are therefore eager to spread capital costs over a metropolitan district, which, according to Abel Wolman, "of course, means that the City of Baltimore would be disproportionately paying for something it doesn't need." After years of study and negotiation, a regional water and sewer authority acceptable to the several technical administrations has been designed, but its political fate is uncertain.

The same kind of structural conflict of interest occurs with respect to public parks. Because recreation is generally a low intensity land use, it seems rational to purchase lower priced peripheral land. But residents of the peripheral counties, owners of cars and private yards and private mortgages, do not yet feel an urgent need for public parks. Fiscal rivalries aggravate public tightfistedness: no community wants to subsidize a recreational resource for its neighbors. Marina owners do not want to provide sewage dumps for boaters, as Anne Arundel County has not provided public sewers and pumping stations on the low lying recreational peninsulas. Baltimore County has resisted developing parks for regional use and concentrated on insuring developer participation in tucked away neighborhood parks. Howward County adopted a comprehensive park plan and appropriated a large sum, but has fallen far short of target rates of acquisition. These are instances of Kevin Cox's argument that collective (environmental) goods will be underproduced and negative externalities (pollution) will be overproduced. In the opinion of experienced observers, metropolitan government does not appear to be politically feasible in the

Baltimore region, but there is a growing tendency to demand new forms of redistribution or "equalization" through state government. The Regional Planning Council (a state agency) has, for example, called for state acquisition of 200,000 acres of open space. In terms of funding and purchase, the state government has served the appetizer—the purchase of the unique Soldiers Delight serpentine barrens for a state park.

In spite of its capricious legislature and councils, Maryland has a long and distinguished tradition in environmental science and engineering. Seventy-five years ago, when the Olmsteds prepared the stream valley park plan and the city built its sewer system and rebuilt its burnt downtown, there was a flowering of many new forms of environmental planning, with the collaboration of public agencies, private citizens, neighborhoods groups, and professionals, notably the geologists, water chemists, oyster biologists, and civil engineers at the young Johns Hopkins University. A Hopkins economist at that time argued that the key to environmental problems was distribution, and the first thing to consider in distribution was the socioeconomic order based on the legal institutions of property. The renewal of public interest in environmental problems since 1970 is important because it is the only area in which Marylanders appear to be challenging the institutions surrounding property and the transfer of property. Environmental problems are essentially "common" problems, not individual ones, and our environmental concerns reflect the idea Richard T. Ely expressed: "Society lives in a condition of solidarity."

The Institutional Neighborhood

There are three-dozen-odd neighborhoods in the Baltimore region. One neighborhood of a thousand has seven men to each woman, only two dozen children, nobody over sixty-four, and no disabled or unemployed. In another neighborhood of 4,000, half are over fifty-six. There are only two men for each three women. A third live alone. In a neighborhood of 2,400, with a comparable portion of elderly, nobody lives alone, and 5 percent have moved in the last five years. In another neighborhood of more than 3,000 people, half are under nineteen, three-quarters are white, three-fifths are male, but only 6 percent are in the labor force. In yet another, of 1,400 residents, nearly all are men, two-thirds black. Three-quarters have moved in recently and a quarter are separated from their wives.

What these five neighborhoods have in common is their institutional character. The first is an army installation, the second adjoins a university, the third is a state mental hospital, the fourth is a training school for the retarded, and the fifth a prison. Each institution is unique, yet they represent a large class of neighborhoods. There are in the region five such military bases (15,000 residents in barracks) including Fort Meade and the U.S. Naval Academy. There are five such large mental hospitals and several smaller ones—9,000 beds. The general hospitals of the region have another 9,000 beds, but turnover is swifter and their occupants are not considered residents. There is a prison population of roughly 6,000, and a comparable number in the dormitories of universities and colleges. Half the 60,000 people classed as living in group quarters are concentrated in these neighborhoods. The rest are in smaller institutions of several hundred, such as the 10,000 in nursing homes and homes for the aged—two-thirds run for profit, one-third nonprofit.

The nonprofit institutions, whether public or private, are an important force in the local economy. The military bases and college campuses are large users of land. The Johns Hopkins medical institutions are one of the largest employers in Baltimore City. As purchasers, they affect specialized sectors such as water use, laundry, laboratories, vending machines, and hotels. They affect neighborhoods in terms of housing markets, parking demand, vehicle traffic, pedestrian movement, and evening or nighttime activity. They also have a privileged position in the tax structure. In the city, 28 percent of land is tax-exempt—or nearly a billion dollars value. About one-third is accounted for by universities, hospitals, schools, and churches, another 40 percent by the city's own enterprises, including the public schools.

Is it reasonable to lump together these institutions with their diverse objectives? Is it reasonable to regard them as residential neighborhoods? Certainly their designers, architects, and managers regard them as specialized residential neighborhoods. They are the ultimate in planned communities. While they reflect to some extent the ideas of specialized professionals in the nation at large, they also reflect political and financial priorities of the local community over many years. They add up to an intricate system which sorts people or differentiates among them and isolates them for longer or shorter periods of time, to greater or lesser degree, from others in the community. In the largest and most isolated institutions— the mental and penal institutions—contrasts of race and sex dramatize the extent to which the assignment of caretakers *in loco parentis* reflects the same pecking order apparent in the labor force and the housing market.

Institutional peculiarities and new thrusts must reflect the peculiar dimensions and dynamics of Baltimore's social life. Changes are taking place in institutional structures, particularly medical, educational, and caretaking services. These are apparent in the geographical arrangement. By looking at the location and relocation patterns, we can discover some aspects of an institutional crisis and, woven into it, a crisis of values. The basic problem is the effectiveness of institutions with respect to their goals in a continually changing society. Like the physical plant itself, the institutional organizational structure tends to become obsolete. In the context of urban geography, the city is changing and moving and institutions must change or move also.

Many hospitals and schools were originally located and designed for a definite type of service and a definite clientele. Baltimore had, for example, a Jewish hospital (Sinai), a German Protestant orphans' home, a farm school for colored boys, a Lithuanian parochial school, a grade school for Irish children (without regard to religion), public "English-German" schools, and so forth. All were created and endowed to respond to certain needs. But what happens when there are no longer many German orphans or no ready markets for black farm labor? What happens when the Jewish population moves to another part of town and the hospital is surrounded by black Protestants? The Baltimore Urban Parish Study is an account of the cumulation of such problems for the parochial elementary schools of the archdiocese.

It is also necessary to appreciate the fiscal context. As a nonprofit service enterprise in a profit-structured society, each organization had built into it some conception of social responsibility, personal responsibility, and common values which could be mobilized to support and pay for the services. These were not easy to organize. At the turn of the century, the creation of a Jewish hospital, recre-

ation center, family and youth services, and charities involved tense alliances between rich and poor, newcomer and establishment, German and Russian, Orthodox and Reformed. (Some of the nuances are described by Isaac M. Fein.) In the 1960s raising $1 million in the Negro community to build a modern building for Provident Hospital has also involved complex tensions and strategic considerations. After the institutions are established, they remain vulnerable. The three-cornered relationship between financial backers, professional managers, and users is continually subject to change. One cannot make the "equilibrium" assumptions of a private enterprise in which interests are automatically reconciled in the balance sheet. All these institutions are initially defined as money losers. The problem lies in the "glue" which holds such machinery together.

PROBLEMS OF SITE
AND ENVIRONMENT

Certain large institutions traditionally preferred large, isolated, suburban or rural tracts. Such sites had the advantages of fresh air and sunshine, and land which could be farmed or pastured to provide work therapy, fresh milk, or economies of growing food. Moreover they provided security, either to protect a vulnerable population of children, youth, retarded, or senile against a threatening society, or to protect society from a threatening population, criminal or contagious.

This pattern of location has produced two types of obsolescence. We shall look at some examples of each, with the several kinds of institutional response or reorganization which followed. The first is the set of remote sites which are no longer suitable for a changed role of the institution in modern society. The state mental hospitals are all in isolated locations which have become handicaps as their philosophy has changed. Visiting is difficult, outpatient treatment and follow-up care are impractical, and employment outside the institution is impossible. In other words, the institutions were located for indefinite or permanent alienation from society and these locations are not easy to adapt to the strategy of reintegrating the individual into normal patterns of work and interaction. Something similar has happened with the tuberculosis hospitals, now that tuberculosis is also largely treated with drugs on an outpatient basis. Juvenile "villages" and houses of correction are also locations of this type.

The new philosophies of treatment have therefore required the creation of a new set of institutions on a smaller scale in the community or close to population centers. The logic is convincing and since 1970 funding has begun in earnest. For example, the state Department of Corrections has plans to decentralize half the prison population into community correction centers of 198 residents each. For delinquent or disturbed youth, several new "group homes" have been organized in the past three years and the intent is to abandon the larger institutions. The state Department of Mental Health has created several specialized outpatient services for psychiatric treatment of alcoholics, drug addicts, and persons prone to violence or suicide, and also several new small scale residential facilities for retarded persons and "halfway" houses for people able to leave the state hospitals.

But the effort to locate all such new facilities has repeatedly come into conflict with the defensive strategies of residential neighborhoods. Their chief resort is the zoning laws. The public continues to regard the people returning from institutions as alien and threatening populations. The facilities so far located are clustered in areas of old mansions and large daytime populations, on the outer fringes of the central business district.

The second type of obsolescence appears where the city has overgrown a remote countrified location, destroyed its rural assets, and hemmed it in with urban traffic, high value land uses, and urban environmental threats. One institutional option was simply to exit (see Albert Hirschman's work), particularly where the traditional clientele had exited or where the users had no clear ties with the neighborhood. For example, most of the colleges, boarding schools, seminaries, and convents moved to larger and greener sites in the suburbs. This process was continuous over 200 years, but there was a notable spurt in the 1950s, leaving an immense amount of under-utilized and ill-maintained social capital behind.

Leaving the truly critical gap, doctors and several hospitals moved out, in response to a mix of more and less rewarded services. Three hundred doctors have private practices in the city, as compared with 950 thirty years ago and 500 now in Baltimore County. A dramatic restructuring of health facilities was inevitable

to compensate for the exits. The large hospitals experienced dramatic expansion of demand in their outpatient clinics and emergency rooms. The phenomenon has been even more severe in Baltimore than other cities. Federal financing contributed to this important shift in the delivery of medical services—Medicare, Medicaid, and HEW construction funds. The rising capital-intensity and specialization of new medical technology also favored the creation of comprehensive pediatric clinics and "primary care" facilities now under construction. These developments help to fill the vacuum in the inner city, but they cluster around established hospital sites precisely the same set of growth poles as for mental health services, halfway houses and services to the aged.

The same type of institutional concentration has appeared in the suburban ring, at Towson (Sheppard-Pratt, Greater Baltimore Medical Center, and Saint Joseph's hospitals adjoin), on the east (Essex Community College and Franklin Square Hospital), and at Catonsville. But the beltway ring sites are relatively favorable to readaptation, on site expansion, and improved access, whereas the most centrally located hospitals, among the oldest and most diversified, have acute problems of site expansion. The University of Maryland (1820), Johns Hopkins Medical Institutions (opened 1891), and, near Mount Vernon, Mercy Hospital (1805) and Maryland General, were once country locations. They are now the favored locations for new services for the core area of public dependency, as well as the highly specialized Metro Center activities in medicine, education, and research. (A trauma center with heliport, for example, has been located at Maryland General.) Urban renewal has been a prime means of delivering land with federal subsidy, notable for the expansion of Johns Hopkins and University of Maryland hospitals. The city's off-street parking commission, formerly concerned with boosting downtown shopping, is now devoting its effort to providing garages for the hospitals.

A CASE OF
INSTITUTIONAL RENEWAL

The exit of institutions required painful adjustment in abandoned communities. But adjustments have also been painful where institutions chose to stay. The case of the Johns Hopkins Hospital is an example of exceptional scale and drama. Successive projects on the perimeter of the Johns Hopkins Medical Institutions in the 1950s produced a medical residence with a small outdoor swimming pool; a fenced-in "compound" for families of medical personnel, with barred windows and playground; a hotel for out-of-town relatives of private patients; and a huge parking garage—all on the site of several thousand dwellings. The evicted residents live in the surrounding area. Most are black, poor, and use the hospital. But the medical personnel were white. This is the premium medical educational institution of the South. Negro doctors and their private patients were not accommodated until the last few years. Since 1965 there has been a rising percentage of Asian immigrant personnel.

Seething resentment came to a boil in the late 1960s over the issue of a black top "football field" which the renewal projects had created for Paul Laurence Dunbar High School (Figure 30). This conflict generated a political movement, a promise of an entirely new school

and multipurpose center, and, to plan it, the extraordinary "Dunbar charette." This was a continuous fourteen day brainstorming effort by a hundred people, including parents, teachers and students from the high school, other representatives from the neighborhood, and personnel from the hospital. From the larger community came others—from the institutions of black leadership—Provident Hospital and Morgan State College—from the archdiocese, city school administration, and federal education consultants, plus the architects and "organizers." As J.H. Harrison reported,

> In the view of the Dunbar community residents, there exists no meaningful community in the Dunbar area. The area is essentially underdeveloped. . . . There is no land available that does not involve someone's dislocation.

The fourteen days were stormy and harried. More important than the innovative character

Figure 30. Dunbar High School. Photo by Julian Olson.

of the building is the vision around which they designed it, of a community that would emerge —not a community within the school, but the Dunbar facility as the focal point of a real neighborhood.

The educational program recommended by the charette involved contract learning, student choices of learning methods, and councils and review boards of the faculty, students, and community. They demanded a strong liberal arts curriculum open to all and a vocational curriculum oriented to growth occupations in which black workers are underrepresented— management, entrepreneurship, sales work, and a unique range of health careers, but not blue collar manufacturing. The hospital is to contribute to the facilities, teaching, motivation, and job opportunities for graduates in the health sector.

The buildings are arranged so that the swimming pool, cafeteria, and movie theatre can be used at different hours by students and others from the community or the public at large. Residents of the entire neighborhood will be served by the information center for job placement, career planning, and occupational counseling. A "neighborhood city hall" was envisioned, with offices for the area's councilmen and voter registration outreach, "to develop in the people of the second ward a feeling of their own political potency".

The Dunbar episode shows how institutional renewal must occur simultaneously on many fronts—in the hospital, in the overall system for delivering medical care, in public education, in political redistricting, in the job market, and in personal soul searching. The painful process of reorganizing and reforming so many institutions took place in the specific geographical context of a neighborhood. The institutional bureaucracies themselves could not have accomplished their renewal individually or jointly. It was their unwilling neighbors who got it together, because the changes required for "neighborhood development" spilled out of the neighborhood. The "glue" which held the charette together through moments of hostility and hours of stalemate was Baltimore's experience of the burning in April 1968, less than a year earlier.

Will the Dunbar effort succeed? The school is operating. The tension still remains between a struggle for "meaningful community" at a neighborhood scale and the pressures on Hop-

kins Hospital to grow and extend on a scale which does not relate to this neighborhood— its citywide children's trauma center, its research of national importance, its surgical pioneering, and its international programs in public health. Hopkins is undertaking a building program which dwarfs the sorely felt renewal of the 1950s. The Hopkins picture is just one example illustrating the neighborhood-battering force of institutional growth. The institutions have burst out of the topographic cadre, out of the pedestrian scale, out of the ethnic scale.

The Dunbar community, in spite of its new physical center and the community experience by which it was obtained, is also caught in a larger structure which severely limits educational opportunities—the whole structure of residential segregation at the scale of the metropolis. In the Park Heights corridor (northwest corner of the city) also, community aspirations and political power have mobilized imagination and talent to rethink and remodel their educational institutions, and there, too, the community is hemmed in by the metropolitan ring and wedge structures which limit the range of variation of pupil experience and family resources. Even at the scale of the whole city, that basic structure remains the stumbling block to all schemes for "desegregation" by race and "equalization" among income groups. The "low level trap" which restricts the job mobility of the work force also constrains the educational development of tomorrow's work force, perpetuating the inequality.

INSTITUTIONAL DECISIONMAKING

Institutional growth must also be seen in the context of metropolitan-scale finance. In the nonprofit institutions, costs are visible and measurable, but the benefits are usually hard to measure. Cost shifts are therefore attentively examined, while shifts in benefits are ignored. Because there is always the risk that the donor will exit, those generous givers often influence decisions. In Baltimore there is a definite control of the boards of nonprofit institutions (whether public or private) by the directors and managers of the financial sector—the banks and utilities. U.S. Congressional Banking Committee hearings (1967) showed a tighter interlocking of directorships among Baltimore banks than for other cities. Manufacturing industries may be underrepresented because so few are home owned and the archdiocese may be closer to the core than in other cities, but the pattern is the usual one of a close knit core of white, male, moneyed respectability, aloof from "politics" and unknown to most people. They live in the green wedge and their close knit web contrasts with the extreme fragmentation of the clienteles or users of the institutions—unevenly assigned by race, religion, means, and residence.

Vigorous and sometimes violent confrontations have dented that power structure in the past ten years. Tenants' councils have been organized in public housing. New appointments were made to the city school board in order to allow parents of public school children to outnumber those who sent their children to private or parochial schools. The city's Civil Service Board was induced to add bonus points for city residence (as for veteran status), because more than a third of the city's policemen, firemen, and hospital employees lived outside the city (coincidental with an underrepresentation of blacks in these jobs). Hospital and university boards have hastened to add token blacks and women, while the financial sector promoted at least one Jewish member into the inner circle of 150. Nevertheless, change does not seem to have touched the core of this structure. Likewise, in the political structure, even the election of a Republican governor in Maryland, his accession to the vice-presidency, and a heavy Republican vote for president in 1972 produced no hint of a viable Republican party in Maryland. Maryland democracy remains a solid one party system of Byzantine intrigue. Many political, professional, and financial roles are, like family businesses, inherited. The extraordinary stability of the financial elite and the political order affects the quality of leadership and the rate of change which can be expected in institutional and social process and, therefore, in the form or pattern of the urban space.

The Image: Does It Matter?

A PLACE TO VISIT

The mayor and business leaders are concerned about the city's image among port users, in international trade, and in national tourism (Figure 31). Baltimore was known for the Preakness and for its sports teams—the Colts, the Orioles, the Bullets, and the Clippers. Does it matter whether the teams are sold to some other town? Which of dozens of promotional schemes—aquarium, floating restaurant, scale model of the harbor, hotel school—will put across a Baltimore image? Will a $100 million stadium make Baltimore more visible? Or will it make it look more like Dallas? Does it matter that the B & O Railroad now calls itself the Chessie, that the excursion boats have no place to go, that a New Orleans decor was proposed for an amusement park in Howard County? Is a police headquarters with golden windows more of an enhancement for the Baltimore image than the famous but seedy "Block" of nightclubs?

Baltimore was simply not built for tourists. To visit Baltimore, you have to look for it. You have to keep moving. Go in search of something—azaleas in May and roses in June, the fringed gentian in November. If you want flag-draped neighborhoods on the Fourth, try Hampden, Locust Point, and Highlandtown. For Christmas decorations, drive through Windsor Hills and Forest Park. If you came in by the Jones Falls Expressway, take the old Falls Road out. Or drive out Wilkins Avenue, and come back in by Washington Boulevard. Every-

thing you visit—Fort McHenry, the B & O railroad museum, the Basilica, the Lexington Market, Mencken's home or Poe's, or Babe Ruth's or Mother Seton's, the pagoda in Patterson Park—grab the chance to explore the neighborhood around it. Stop in for a soda or a coffee or a beer on the corner and let yourself get drawn into the banter and the warmth. Because Baltimore is a place to live. As one citizen at an expressway hearing put it,

> I say first the city is a place to live in. They say first the city is a place to make money in. Whether I am right or they are right makes the big difference.

A PLACE TO LIVE

What kind of image do we have of ourselves? Does it matter that we have no hometown firms, that we work for Bethlehem, but Bethlehem's identity isn't Baltimore? Must our productive power be a massive secret all around us? Must every factory be surrounded by parking lots and cyclone fences? Must our port remain invisible?

And why shouldn't we be proud of taking in each other's washing? The quickest way to get a grasp of our dependence on each other is to spend Saturday night in the emergency room. Does it matter that our hospitals look like penitentiaries and that operating room lighting has been extended to the streets around them?

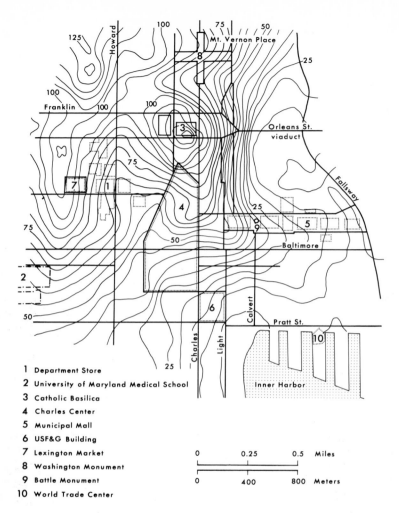

1 Department Store
2 University of Maryland Medical School
3 Catholic Basilica
4 Charles Center
5 Municipal Mall
6 USF&G Building
7 Lexington Market
8 Washington Monument
9 Battle Monument
10 World Trade Center

Figure 31. Downtown in 3-D. The generation of the War in 1812 saw the rugged topography of Baltimore as a stage for architectural monuments—the Catholic Basilica, the Washington Monument, the Battle Monument, the University of Maryland medical school, and the Lexington Market. A "progressive" and efficiency-minded generation 100 years later took advantage of terrain for a municipal mall, a sewer system, the Fallsway (over Jones Falls), and the Orleans Street viaduct. The generation of the 1960s used the terrain of Charles Center for walkways above traffic, underground parking, and vistas of the older monuments. They have designed a waterfront skyline with two new monuments to finance and trade: The USF&G building has forty stories, the World Trade Center will have thirty-two. The department store gully is still unreclaimed.

Baltimore still has a potential for integrity in its fine scale or grain. Baltimore is not part of the Roman Empire, in spite of the grandoise office schemes of the federal and state governments. In the neighborhoods, street life depends on the scale of the streets and houses. Even the downtown has a neighborhood quality. Charles Center, compared with such projects in other downtowns, is intimate and fits

into a pieced-together fabric of buildings of eight generations—the rectory of Saint Paul's, the steeple of Saint Alphonsus, the Shot Tower, the Basilica. In order to be itself, Baltimore must, like New England, accept its own provincialism and revel in its patchwork.

H.L. Mencken, one of Baltimore's orneriest citizens, appealed to that sense of identity and integrity of Baltimore's self-image. In the 1910s he argued for beer and Sunday concerts. In the 1920s he ranted against filling stations and suburban houses (no privacy) and the so-called skyscrapers: "There was never any need of them here." In the thirties he vented his spleen on the east-west viaduct.

Wasting millions on such follies is simply not Baltimorish. Every enterprise of the sort is a kind of confession that Baltimore is inferior to New York, and should hump itself to catch up. No true Baltimorean believes that. He accepts the difference between a provincial capital and a national metropolis as natural and inevitable, and he sees no reason why any effort should be made to conceal it. He lives in Baltimore because he prefers Baltimore. One of its

Figure 32. Kids running, the dome of city hall, a patchwork of downtown land uses.

greatest charms, in his eyes, is that it is not New York.

Studding the inner city are symbols of its ethnic patchwork. Baltimore's social mix differs from Boston or New York or Cleveland or Los Angeles, just as their mix of industry differs and their house types differ. Two blocks from the Baltimore Symphony is the Left Bank Jazz Society. By a hair's breadth, the Jewish community saved the Lloyd Street Synagogue and the Sulpicians restored St. Mary's Chapel before they moved out of the seminary. Each of those buildings has the power to communicate the sense of prayer by which a whole community survived and each is a doorway to one of Baltimore's hidden worlds. Does it matter that one is only open one afternoon a month, the other never? "Beautiful Baltimore" and "Black is Beautiful" are slogans of the moment. The third term—"Baltimore is Black" —is rarely posted. Blacks made the bricks and blacks keep downtown alive, but their aspirations, generation after generation, need stronger symbols at the center (Figure 32).

A PLACE TO GROW

Baltimore neighborhoods are a wonderful radius of action for a child. Hopscotches are drawn like nowhere else. We eat sauerkraut with our Thanksgiving turkey and black-eyed peas for New Year's. We all go out on new roller skates on Christmas even if it snows, and visit the "Christmas garden"—model railroad displays at the firehouse. We take in the state fair in August, the City fair in September, the Fell's Point Fair in October, and all the lesser street fairs.

But what happens when you outgrow the neighborhood? There is the new "undistricted" high school complex of 4,000 students. What kind of neighborhood is that? In Locust Point and Canton some of the boys still slip out of childhood right into a warm spot next to dad at the tavern and the hiring hall. Some of the girls still move from courting on mom's front steps to scrubbing their own white stoop three doors down or around the corner. But not so many. The adolescent and the newcomer share a need for an arena, a smithy in which to forge identity and solidarity. Although the region has 40,000 full time college students, it lacks a student quarter and consequently has no bookstore, no home for political life, mature artistic life, or ideological debate. Mount Vernon Place has some potential, but escapes its old gentility only by perennial outrage. The Maryland Institute of Art had a vision when they bought Mount Royal Station (B & O), but the state has now, by design or default, acquired most of the surrounding land and shows no sign of grasping that vision. Fell's Point may yet survive the highway project, now scheduled to be "sunk" in the mud off the point, but designs for the Inner Harbor East campus of the Community College of Baltimore appear to be as sterile as the University of Maryland complex.

Meanwhile, the place to discover Baltimore and discover yourself is at public meetings. Nineteenth century Baltimoreans loved public hangings, town meetings, and the hustings. Officially, jousting is the state sport, but in fact the courtroom is from colonial days to this moment the real Maryland jousting place and our favorite source of gossip. One can also rely on daytime attractions at the School Board, the Liquor Board, and the Board of Zoning Appeals. Baltimore's public life is an emotional rollercoaster. Urban renewal community meetings offer nightly guerrilla theatre. Expressway hearings and cycle zoning hearings in the counties are less frequent but clearly polarized: you won't need a score card to tell the players. The observer should be warned, however, of the risk of involvement. The candor and the vehemence are contagious. People rarely succeed in remaining neutral.

Bibliography

Amourgis, Spyros. "Baltimore—A Design Concept for the Inner Core of the City." Occasional paper of the Johns Hopkins University Center for Metropolitan Planning and Research, 1975.

Archdiocese of Baltimore. *Baltimore Urban Parish Study*. Baltimore, 1967.

Associated Jewish Charities of Baltimore. *The Jewish Community of Greater Baltimore, a Population Study*. December 26, 1968.

Bachrach, Peter, and Baratz, Morton S. *Power and Poverty, Theory and Practice*. Oxford University Press, 1970.

Baltimore Citizens Planning and Housing Association. *Bawlamer, an Informal Guide to a Livelier Baltimore*. 1971.

Baltimore City. *Municipal Handbook*. 1969.

Baltimore City. Department of Housing and Community Development. *Annual Reports*.

———. *Oldtown Development Guide and Upton Development Guide*. August 1970.

Baltimore City. Department of Planning, and Johns Hopkins University Center for Urban Affairs. *Census Notes*. Irregular issues, 1971.

Batimore City. Urban Renewal and Housing Agency. *Displacement and Relocation, Past and Future, Baltimore, Maryland*. Stage one staff monograph 5.4, March 1965.

———. *Harlem Park, a Demonstration of Rehabilitation*. June 1965.

Baltimore Sun, 1961–1973.

Baltimore Evening Sun.

Baltimore New American.

Barker, Constance L. *Relocation and the Housing Market in Metropolitan Baltimore, 1968–1975*. Regional Planning Council, 1968.

Beck, Alan M. *The Ecology of Stray Dogs, A Study of Free-Ranging Urban Animals*. Baltimore: York Press, 1973.

Bedini, Silvio A. *The Life of Benjamin Banneker*. Scribner's, 1972.

Bennett, Robert R., and Meyer, Rex R. *Geology and Ground Water Resources of the Baltimore Area*. Maryland Geologic Survey bulletin no. 4. 1952.

Chatterjee, Lata; Harvey, David; and Klugman, Lawrence. *FHA Policies and the Baltimore City Housing Market*. Baltimore: The Urban Observatory, April 1974.

Council of Churches and Christian Education of Maryland and Delaware. *The Negro Church in Baltimore*. 1934.

Crenson, Matthew. *Survey of Organized Citizen Participation in Baltimore, Final Report*. Baltimore Urban Observatory, Inc.

Crooks, James B. *Politics and Progress, the Rise of Urban Progressivism in Baltimore, 1895 to 1911*. Louisiana State University Press, 1968.

Educational Facilities Laboratory. *Experiment in Planning an Urban High School: The Baltimore Charette*. Case Studies no. 13. 1969.

Ely, Richard T. *Property and Contract in their Relation to the Distribution of Wealth*. Boston: Thomas Crowell, 1914.

Emmart, William W. "Report on Housing and Commercial Conditions in Baltimore." Studies prepared for Mayor Howard W. Jackson, October 1934 (Municipal Reference Library).

Fein, Isaac M. *The Making of an American Jewish Community, the History of Baltimore*

Jewry from 1773 to 1920. Philadelphia: Jewish Publication Society of America, 1971.

Feld, Joseph A. "The Changing Geography of Baltimore Jewry." Paper, Johns Jopkins University, August 1968.

Geyer, John C. *Ground Water in the Baltimore Industrial Area.* Maryland State Planning Commission, publication no. 44, May 1945.

Gottschalk, L.C. "Effects of Soil Erosion on Navigation in Upper Chesapeake Bay." *Geographical Review* (1945), pp. 219–38.

———. Sedimentation in a Great Harbor. *Soil Conservation* 10, 1 (July 1944): 3–5, 11–12.

Haeuber, Douglas H. "The Baltimore Expressway Controversy: A Study of the Political Decision-Making Process." Occasional Paper, The Johns Hopkins University Center for Metropolitan Planning and Research, 1974.

Harrison, James Haywood, ed. *People, Planning, and Community and the Creation of a New Paul Laurence Dunbar High School in Baltimore, Maryland.* March 1969.

Harvey, David. *Class-Monopoly Rent, Finance Capital and the Urban Revolution.* University of Toronto, Department of Urban and Regional Planning, Papers on Planning and Design, no. 4. March 1974.

———. *Social Justice and the City.* London: Edwin Arnold, 1973.

Harvey, David, and Chatterjee, Lata. "Absolute Rent and the Structuring of Space by Governmental and Financial Institutions." *Antipode* 6, 1 (April 1974): 22–36.

Harvey, David, et al. *The Housing Market and Code Enforcement in Baltimore.* The Baltimore Urban Observatory, Inc., City Planning Department, July 1972.

Hirschfeld, Charles. *Baltimore, 1870–1900: Studies in Social History.* Baltimore: Johns Hopkins Press, 1941.

Hirschman, Albert O. *Exit, Voice and Loyalty.* Cambridge, Mass.: Harvard University Press, 1970.

Keller, Suzanne. *The Urban Neighborhood: A Sociological Perspective.* Randon House, 1968.

Laumann, Edward O. *Bonds of Pluralism: the Form and Substance of Urban Social Networks.* John Wiley, 1973.

Marx, Karl. *Grundrisse.* Translation of Martin Nicolaus. Pelican 1973.

Maryland, Department of State Planning. *Maryland Chesapeake Bay Study, Report.* Wallace McHarg Roberts and Todd, Inc., March 1972.

Maryland Geologic Survey. Topographic Maps of Baltimore County and Anne Arundel County.

Maryland Historical Magazine.

Maryland, Regional Planning Council. *General Development Plan for the Baltimore Region.* September 1972.

Maryland, Regional Planning Council, and the Baltimore City Department of Planning. *MetroCenter/Baltimore, technical study.* Wallace, McHarg, Roberts and Todd, 1970.

Maryland, State Planning Commission, Baltimore Regional Planning Council. *Water Supply and Sewerage.* Technical Report no. 4. May 1959.

Mason, T.J., and McKay, F.W. *U.S. Cancer Mortality by County, 1950–1969.* Bethesda, Md.: Department of Health, Education and Welfare, Pub. no. (NIH) 74–514, 1975.

National Education Association. *Baltimore, Maryland, Change and Contrast—the Children and the Public Schools.* Washington, D.C., May 1967.

Olmsted Brothers. *Development of Public Grounds for Greater Baltimore.* 1904.

Porter, John. *The Vertical Mosaic, an Analysis of Social Class and Power in Canada.* Toronto: University of Toronto Press, 1965.

Radford, Edward P. "Cancer Mortality in the Steel Industry." Paper presented at Conference on Occupational Carcinogenesis, New York Academy of Sciences, March 27, 1975. mimeographed.

Reutter, Mark. "The Endless Road: Baltimore's Expressway Controversy." Paper, April 16, 1973.

Rothman, David J. *The Discovery of the Asylum.* Boston: Little, Brown, 1971.

Sennett, Richard. *The Uses of Disorder: Personal Identity and City Life.* Vintage, 1970.

Snow, Raymond W., and Frazier, Andrew S. "Racial Development of the Pennsylvania-Eutaw Corridor." Paper, Johns Hopkins University, December 1969.

Sober, Marc. "The Baptist Churches of Baltimore." Paper, Johns Hopkins University, December 1969.

Stanton, Phoebe B. *The Gothic Revival*

and American Church Architecture. Baltimore: Johns Hopkins Press, 1968.

Thomas, Brinley. *Migration and Urban Development.* Methuen, 1972.

University of Maryland. Cooperative Extension Service. *Maryland Soils.* Bulletin 212, May 1967.

Urban Design Concept Associates. *Segment Area Reports,* November 1, 1968; *Point III Reports,* July 1970; and *Roadway Corridor Design, Baltimore Highway System 3-A,* December 1970. prepared for Maryland State Roads Commission and Interstate Division for Baltimore City.

U.S. Commission on Civil Rights, Maryland State Advisory Committee. *Transcript of Hearings, Baltimore, Maryland, January 1971.*

U.S., Congress, House. Committee on Banking and Currency. Control of Commercial Banks and Interlocks among Financial Institutions. 90th Cong., 1st sess. Staff Report, July 31, 1967.

Waesche, James F. *Baltimore Today . . . A Guide to its Pleasures, Treasures, and Past.* Bodine and Associates, Inc., 1969.

Wallace, David A., and McDonnell, William C. "Diary of a Plan." *Journal of the American Institute of Planners* 37, 1 (January 1971): 11–25.

Wallace-McHarg Associates. *A Plan for the Valleys.* 1964.

Whitman, Ira L. *Physical Condition of Streams in Baltimore and Their Relation to Park Areas.* Report to Departments of Recreation and Parks, and Public Works, Baltimore, December 1966.

Wolman, Abel, and Hoffman, Janet. Interviews in *Metro News* (Johns Hopkins University Center for Metropolitan Planning and Research) 3, 1 (September 15, 1974.)

Wolman, M. Gordon. "A Cycle of Sedimentation and Erosion in Urban River Channels." *Geografiska Annaler,* 49 Series A, 2, 4 (1967): 385–95.

About the Author

Sherry H. Olson, a former resident of the Baltimore area, received her M.A. and Ph.D. in Geography from Johns Hopkins University. She subsequently taught at Johns Hopkins for seven years. She is currently an Associate Professor of Geography at McGill University.